DESIGNING AND
CONDUCTING
ETHNOGRAPHIC

ONE WEEK

ETHNOGRAPHER'S TOOLKIT

Edited by Jean J. Schensul, *Institute for Community Research, Hartford,* and
Margaret D. LeCompte, *School of Education, University of Colorado, Boulder*

The **Ethnographer's Toolkit** is designed with you, the novice fieldworker, in mind. In a series of seven brief books, the editors and authors of the **Toolkit** take you through the multiple, complex steps of doing ethnographic research in simple, reader-friendly language. Case studies, checklists, key points to remember, and additional resources to consult are all included to help the reader fully understand the ethnographic process. Eschewing a step-by-step formula approach, the authors are able to explain the complicated tasks and relationships that occur in the field in clear, helpful ways. Research designs, data collection techniques, analytical strategies, research collaborations, and an array of uses for ethnographic work in policy, programming, and practice are described in the volumes. The **Toolkit** is the perfect starting point for professionals in diverse fields including social welfare, education, health, economic development, and the arts, as well as for advanced students and experienced researchers unfamiliar with the demands of conducting good ethnography.

Summer 1999/7 volumes/paperback boxed set/0-7619-9042-9

BOOKS IN THE ETHNOGRAPHER'S TOOLKIT

1. **Designing and Conducting Ethnographic Research,** by Margaret D. LeCompte and Jean J. Schensul, 0-7619-8975-7 (paperback)

2. **Essential Ethnographic Methods: Observations, Interviews, and Questionnaires,** by Stephen Schensul, Jean J. Schensul, and Margaret D. LeCompte, 0-7619-9144-1 (paperback)

3. **Enhanced Ethnographic Methods: Audiovisual Techniques, Focused Group Interviews, and Elicitation Techniques,** by Jean J. Schensul, Margaret D. LeCompte, Bonnie K. Nastasi, and Stephen P. Borgatti, 0-7619-9129-8 (paperback)

4. **Mapping Social Networks, Spatial Data, and Hidden Populations,** by Jean J. Schensul, Margaret D. LeCompte, Robert T. Trotter II, Ellen K. Cromley, and Merrill Singer, 0-7619-9112-3 (paperback)

5. **Analyzing and Interpreting Ethnographic Data,** by Margaret D. LeCompte and Jean J. Schensul, 0-7619-8974-9 (paperback)

6. **Researcher Roles and Research Partnerships,** by Margaret D. LeCompte, Jean J. Schensul, Margaret R. Weeks, and Merrill Singer, 0-7619-8973-0 (paperback)

7. **Using Ethnographic Data: Interventions, Public Programming, and Public Policy,** by Jean J. Schensul, Margaret D. LeCompte, G. Alfred Hess, Jr., Bonnie K. Nastasi, Marlene J. Berg, Lynne Williamson, Jeremy Brecher, and Ruth Glasser, 0-7619-8972-2 (paperback)

DESIGNING & CONDUCTING ETHNOGRAPHIC RESEARCH

MARGARET D. LeCOMPTE
JEAN J. SCHENSUL

1 ETHNOGRAPHER'S TOOLKIT

ALTAMIRA
PRESS

A Division of
ROWMAN & LITTLEFIELD PUBLISHERS, INC.
Walnut Creek • Lanham • New York • Oxford

ALTAMIRA PRESS
A Division of Rowman & Littlefield Publishers, Inc.
1630 North Main Street, #367
Walnut Creek, CA 94596
www.altamirapress.com

Rowman & Littlefield Publishers, Inc.
4720 Boston Way
Lanham, MD 20706

12 Hid's Copse Road
Cumnor Hill, Oxford OX2 9JJ, England

British Library Cataloguing in Publication Information Available

Library of Congress Cataloging-in-Publication Data

LeCompte, Margaret D.
  Designing and conducting ethnographic research / by Margaret D. LeCompte and
Jean J. Schensul.
    p. cm. — (Ethnographer's toolkit; v. 1)
  Includes bibliographical references and index.
  ISBN 0-7619-8975-7 (pbk.)
    1. Ethnology—Evaluation. 2. Ethnology—Methodology. 3. Research—
Evaluation. I. Schensul, Jean J. II. Title. III. Series.
GN345.S35 1999
305.8'0072—dc21   98-40070

Printed in the United States of America

♾™ The paper used in this publication meets the minimum requirements of American
National Standard for Information Sciences—Permanence of Paper for Printed Library
Materials, ANSI/NISO Z39.48–1992.

CONTENTS

LIST OF TABLES AND FIGURES

LIST OF EXAMPLES

INTRODUCTION

The **Ethnographer's Toolkit** is a series of texts on how to plan, design, carry out, and use the results of applied ethnographic research. Ethnography, as an approach to research, may be unfamiliar to people accustomed to more traditional forms of research, but we believe that applied ethnography will prove not only congenial but essential to both researchers and practitioners. Many kinds of evaluative or investigative questions that arise in the course of program planning and implementation cannot really be answered very well with standard research methods, such as experiments or collection of quantifiable data alone. Often, there are no data yet to quantify nor programs whose effectiveness needs to be assessed! Sometimes, the research problem to be addressed is not yet clearly identified and must be discovered. In such cases, ethnographic research provides a valid and important way to find out what *is* happening in programs and to help practitioners plan their activities.

This book series defines what ethnographic research is, when it should be used, and how it can be used to identify and solve complex social problems, especially those not readily amenable to traditional quantitative or experimental research methods alone. It is designed for educators; service professionals; professors of applied students in the fields of teaching, social and health services, communications, engineering, and business; and students working in applied field settings.

Ethnography is a peculiarly human endeavor. Many of its practitioners have commented that, unlike other approaches to research, the *researcher* is the primary tool for collecting primary data. That is, as Books 1, 2, 3, and 4 demonstrate, the ethnographer's principal database is amassed in the course of human interaction: direct observation; face-to-face interviewing and elicitation; audiovisual recording; and mapping the networks, times, and places in which human interactions occur. Thus, as Book 6 makes clear, the personal characteristics and activities of researchers as human beings and as scientists become salient in ways not applicable in research where the investigator maintains more distance from the people and phenomena under study.

Book 1 of the **Ethnographer's Toolkit**, *Designing and Conducting Ethnographic Research,* defines what ethnographic research is and the predominant viewpoints or paradigms that guide ethnography. It provides the reader with an overview of research methods and design, including how to develop research questions, what to consider in setting up the mechanics of a research project, and how to devise a sampling plan. Ways of collecting and analyzing data, and the ethical considerations for which ethnographers must account conclude this overall introduction to the series.

In Book 2, *Essential Ethnographic Methods,* readers are provided with an introduction to participant and nonparticipant observation, interviewing, and ethnographically informed survey research, including systematically administered structured interviews and questionnaires. These data collection strategies are fundamental to good ethnographic research. The essential methods provide ethnographers with tools to answer the principal ethnographic questions: "What's happening in this setting?" "Who is engaging in what kind of activities?" and "Why are they doing what they are doing?" Ethnographers use these tools to enter a field situation and obtain basic information about social structure, social events, cultural patterns, and the meanings people give to these patterns. The essential tools also permit ethnographers to learn about new situations from the perspective of "insiders" because they require ethnographers to become involved in the local cultural setting and to acquire their knowledge through hands-on experience.

In Book 3, *Enhanced Ethnographic Methods,* the reader adds to this basic inventory of ethnographic tools three different but important approaches to data collection, each one a complement to the essential methods presented in Book 2. These tools are audiovisual techniques, focus group interviews, and elicitation techniques. We have termed these data collection strategies "enhanced ethnographic methods" because each of them parallels and enhances a strategy first presented in Book 2.

Audiovisual techniques, which involve recording behavior and speech using electronic equipment, expand the capacity of ethnographers to observe and listen by creating a more complete and permanent record of events and speech. Focus group interviews permit ethnographers to interview more than one person at a time. Elicitation techniques allow ethnographers to quantify qualitative or perceptual data on how individuals and groups of people think about and organize perceptions of their cultural world.

It is important for the reader to recognize that, although the essential ethnographic methods described in Book 2 can be used alone, the enhanced ethnographic methods covered in Book 3 cannot, by themselves, provide a fully rounded picture of cultural life in a community, organization, work group, school, or other setting. Instead, they must be used in combination with the essential methods outlined in Book 2. Doing so adds dimensions of depth and accuracy to the cultural portrait constructed by the ethnographer.

In Book 4, *Mapping Social Networks, Spatial Data, and Hidden Populations,* we add to the enhanced methods of data collection and analysis used by ethnographers. However, the approach taken in Book 4 is informed by a somewhat different perspective on the way social life is organized in communities. Whereas the previous books focus primarily on ways of understanding cultural patterns and the interactions of individuals and groups in cultural settings, Book 4 focuses on how social networks and patterns of interaction, as well as the uses of what we term "socio-geographic space," influence human behavior and beliefs. It also addresses a little-discussed problem in the social sciences: how to locate and study groups of people who, like the homeless or dropouts from school, are, by definition, difficult to find using ordinary selection strategies.

Book 5, *Analyzing and Interpreting Ethnographic Data,* provides the reader with a variety of methods for transforming piles of fieldnotes, observations, audio- and video-tapes, questionnaires, surveys, documents, maps, and other kinds of data into research results that help people to understand their world more fully and to facilitate problem solving. Addressing both narrative and qualitative, as well as quantitative—or enumerated—data, Book 5 discusses methods for organizing, retrieving, rendering manageable, and interpreting the data collected in ethnographic research.

In Book 6, *Researcher Roles and Research Partnerships,* we discuss the special requirements which doing ethnographic research imposes on its practitioners. Throughout the **Ethnographer's Toolkit** series, we have argued that there is little difference between the exercise of ethnography as a systematic and scientific enterprise and applied ethnography, as that same systematic and scientific enterprise used specifically for helping people identify and solve human problems. To that end, in Chapter 1, "Researcher Roles," we first describe how the work of ethnographers is inextricably tied to the type of person the ethnographer is, the particular social and cultural context of the research site, and the tasks and responsibilities that ethnographrs assume in the field.

In the second chapter, "Building Research Partnerships," we recognize that ethnography seldom is done by lone researchers by discussing how ethnographers assemble research teams, establish partnerships with individuals and institutions in the field, and work collaboratively with a wide range of people and organizations to solve mutually identified problems. The chapter concludes with ethical and procedural considerations including developing social and managerial infrastructure, establishing and breaking contracts, negotiating different organizational cultures and values, and resolving conflicts.

The final book in the series, *Using Ethnographic Data: Interventions, Public Programmimg, and Public Policy,* consists of three chapters that present general guidelines and case studies illustrating how ethnographers have used ethnographic data in developing and evaluating interventions, planning public programs, and influencing public policy.

Throughout the series, authors give examples drawn from their own work and the work of their associates. These examples and case studies present ways in which ethnographers have coped with the kinds of problems and dilemmas found in the field—and described in the series—in the course of their work and over extended periods of time.

Readers less familiar with ethnographic research will gain an introduction to basic ethnographic principles, methods, and techniques by reading Books 1, 2, 5, and 6 first, followed by other books that explore more specialized areas of research and use. Those familiar with basic ethnographic methods will find Books 3, 4, and 7 valuable in enhancing their repertoires of research methods, data collection techniques, and ways of approaching the use of ethnographic data in policy and program settings.

This book, *Designing and Conducting Ethnographic Research,* is an introduction to some of the critical concepts underlying the **Ethnographer's Toolkit**—namely "ethnography," "culture," "context," "ethnographic research methods," "research roles and partnerships," "ethnographic data analysis," and "dissemination and use of research results." It is organized into nine chapters, following the major themes addressed in the book series. Chapter 1 defines ethnography and its relationship to concepts of culture, power, gender, race, and ethnicity. Chapter 2 outlines where and when ethnography is best used in research projects. Chapter 3 presents the major conceptual paradigms or ways of thinking in ethnographic research. These paradigms are important to understand because they influence the ways in which research topics are chosen and research questions are framed.

Chapter 4 is an overview of research designs in general, and it places ethnography in relation to research approaches ranging from experiments to rapid assessment. It also indicates how ethnography is used in conjunction with a variety of other researcher designs. Chapter 5 discusses the design of an ethnography, with particular attention to logistical issues and sampling. Chapter 6 is a brief overview of data collection strategies, and Chapter 7 summarizes how ethnographers analyze their data. In the final two chapters, we provide an outline of the personal and professional qualities required to do ethnography and the formal and informal ethical considerations that are incumbent upon researchers to undertake ethnographic projects. In these chapters, we discuss the role and responsibilities of the individual researcher working in institutional or community settings. Recognizing that ethnographic researchers also work with others, this section also reviews the kinds of partnerships that ethnographic researchers can build and their purposes.

We also raise important questions for researchers and their partners with respect to the ethics of applied ethnographic research. This topic is important because ethnography creates new challenges for the ethics of field research practice. The intimacy of relationships established between researchers and their partners and the demands that flow from that intimacy—the continuous interaction with participants, the repeated interviewing typical of ethnographic research, and the long-term contact with research participants—all offer new potential for revealing confidential information and create new demands on researchers for responding to respondent and community needs.

—Jean J. Schensul and Margaret D. LeCompte

1 ━◆━◆━◆

WHAT IS ETHNOGRAPHY?

ETHNOGRAPHY AS SCIENCE

Ethnography is an approach to learning about the social and cultural life of communities, institutions, and other settings that

- Is scientific
- Is investigative
- Uses the researcher as the primary tool of data collection
- Uses rigorous research methods and data collection techniques to avoid bias and ensure accuracy of data
- Emphasizes and builds on the perspectives of the people in the research setting
- Is inductive, building local theories for testing and adapting them for use both locally and elsewhere

Ethnography takes the position that human behavior and the ways in which people construct and make meaning of their worlds and their lives are highly variable and **locally specific.** One primary difference between *ethnography as science* and other social and behavioral science methods of investigation is that ethnography assumes that we must first discover *what* people actually do and the reasons they give

Definition: Locally specific meanings and behavior are those that originate in and are found in one specific location

1

for doing it before we can assign to their actions interpretations drawn from our own personal experience or from our professional or academic disciplines. That is why the tools of ethnography are designed for discovery. The basic tools of ethnography use the researcher's eyes and ears as the primary modes for data collection. Much like naturalists, ethnographic researchers learn through systematic observation in the field by interviewing and carefully recording what they see and hear, as well as how things are done, while learning the meanings that people attribute to what they make and do. The idea that the researcher is the primary tool for data collection may not be comfortable for those who believe that science is "objective" and that the presence and interaction of the researcher in the field may bias the results. For this reason, in this book and subsequent volumes of the **Ethnographer's Toolkit**, we rigorously define the approaches to data collection that ethnographers use. These definitions—the codification of ethnographic research methods—represent an effort to ensure that researchers gather data carefully, thoroughly, and in a way that is understandable to others, and that they use procedures that can be replicated by other researchers even though the field situation may change. This rigor is what helps to produce scientifically valid and reliable data.

A second primary difference between ethnography and other social and behavioral sciences is that ethnographic researchers cannot control what happens in their field situation of choice. Scientific ethnographic research is conducted in field settings where the researcher enters as an "invited guest" to learn what is going on. Thus, the ethnographic field situation is unlike clinic- or laboratory-based experimental research, where most aspects of the environment are controlled and where researchers can use the same **instruments** and can expect to get the same results if the study is repeated. Even when ethnographers use the same instruments, changing circumstances beyond the ethnog-

Definition: Instruments are the tools, including questionnaires and lists of interview questions, that researchers use to collect their data

raphers' control may generate different results that they must be able to explain. In addition, ethnographers may find that a community has changed so much that using the same instruments as in a previous study now is inappropriate. For example, if the population of a community changes from one that is primarily Mexican and Spanish-speaking to one that is primarily Russian and Russian-speaking, the instruments might have to be not only translated but also adapted to suit the different cultures involved.

Lack of control over the field setting is a second concern to those who consider ethnography to be more of an art than a science. What is important to ethnographers as social scientists is their ability to adapt or create locally appropriate aids to data collection or instruments that are effective in building a picture, narrative, story, or theory of local culture that is predictive, at least in the short run, and produces hunches, guesses, and hypotheses that can be applied to the same situation or to other similar situations using the same research methods and data collection techniques.

Ethnographers do not shy away from surveys and other instruments that are used to test concepts and theories derived from other fields or from "outsider" observations. But ethnographers will take the position, consistent with their belief in the integrity of local cultures, that such instruments and the theories that usually direct their use should not be arbitrarily used without testing them locally for both practical applicability (i.e., Do local people understand the language and ideas used by the ethnographer?) and theoretical applicability (i.e., Do the theories that guide these instruments have meaning in the local setting?). Increasingly, this position is coming to be shared by members of other disciplines who historically have held strong beliefs in the generalizability and universality of human behaviors, motivations, and beliefs. Growing understanding of the importance of local culture as the context for research and intervention has helped to increase the visibility and perceived value of ethnography as an alternative scientific approach to research over the past decade (see Bernard, 1995; Pelto & Pelto, 1978; Singer, 1990; Trotter & Schensul, 1998).

Ethnography is often mistaken for qualitative research. *Qualitative research* is a term used to describe *any* research that uses the wide variety of qualitative data collection techniques available, many of which we will describe in detail in Books 2, 3, and 4 of this series. Qualitative research can be descriptive, used as part of a quantitative research design, or used in the development of quantitative measures. By contrast, ethnography can be and do all of these things, but it is both more and less than qualitative research.

Cross Reference: Ethnographic methods are described in detail in Books 2, 3, and 4

The Historical Development of Ethnography

Historically, ethnography has been thought of as both a product of research and a research process (LeCompte & Preissle, 1993). The product is an interpretive story, reconstruction, or narrative about a group of people (a community). It includes some historical material and paints a picture of people going about their daily lives as they happen over a relatively representative period of time. The content of an ethnography can address some or all of the following: beliefs; attitudes; perceptions; emotions; verbal and nonverbal means of communication; social networks; behaviors of the group of individuals with friends, family, associates, fellow workers, and colleagues; use of tools; technology and manufacture of materials and artifacts; and patterned use of space and time.

The ethnographic research process involves longer term, face-to-face interaction with people in the research community using the tools of data collection described in Books 2, 3, and 4. Earlier in the 20th century, ethnographers lived in a community for up to 2 or 3 years, learning about as many aspects of community life as possible. Nowadays, ethnographers work for shorter periods of time in communities of varying size and complexity, and in institutions that may be local, regional, national, or global. Contemporary ethnographies generally are focused on a particular aspect or dimension of culture simply because it is no longer possible for most researchers to spend years in a single site. In addition, contemporary ethnography tends to be problem oriented, addressing specific issues or problems in a community context, which also serves to narrow and focus the research endeavor.

To accomplish high-quality ethnographic research despite relatively brief periods of research time and limited resources, researchers restrict their studies to a topic or "lens" through which to view the community they are studying. Thus, for example, an educator may choose to conduct ethnographic research with Puerto Rican families and educators in the schools their children attend, but restrict the research focus to inquiring why Puerto Rican children are enrolling in school well after opening day. Or staff of a nonprofit organization serving pregnant young women may conduct an ethnographic study focusing on social supports available to these young women after they give birth, rather than considering the full scope of their reproductive health concerns.

Ethnography for Problem Identification and Solving

Although this series can be used by anyone interested in learning how to conduct ethnographic research, we specifically emphasize the application of ethnographic research to the solution of human problems. Some researchers make a distinction between research applied to solving human problems—calling it *applied* research—and research designed to answer questions without reference to solving any problems—calling it *basic* research. This does not mean that basic research cannot be used in solving problems; in fact, it usually is. However, applied research also is specifically directed toward bringing about a change in the circumstances of people involved in the research project. In the **Ethnographer's Toolkit,** we are discussing how to design and carry out research projects. We have tended to use the terms "applied ethnographic research" and "ethnographic research" synonymously because we believe strongly that the same rules for systematic and rigorous work apply to both. That being said, we also want to make clear that the purposes of **applied ethnographic research** are always centered on two goals:

Definition: Applied ethnographic research is concerned with understanding sociocultural problems and using these understandings to bring about positive change in communities, institutions, or groups

- Understanding sociocultural problems in communities or institutions
- Using the research to solve problems or help bring about positive change in institutions or communities

The problem to be investigated is always identified in advance by researchers working with partners in the place where the study is to be carried out. The problem guides the study even though the study may conclude with a complete redefinition of the problem. Both the problem and the study itself must be negotiated within a particular community or social context whose members control whether or not research will be done and, often, how the results will be used. If the problem identified by the ethnographer is viewed as important by community leaders, members, or **gatekeepers,** or if the problem is identified by the community or institution itself, the researcher will find it easy to gain entry to the research setting. On the other hand, if the problem is viewed as unimportant, or if the study is perceived to be a threat to community unity, the researcher will have difficulty gaining entry. The following examples illustrate these points.

Definition: Gatekeepers are individuals who control access to a community, organization, group of people, or source of information

EXAMPLE 1.1

DEFINING PROBLEMS IN A NAVAJO COMMUNITY

Over a period of several years, Margaret LeCompte conducted a study of reform efforts in a school district in the Navajo Nation, which is located in an extremely rural and isolated southwestern region of the United States. After considerable fieldwork, it became clear to her and to several of the high school teachers that reforming curriculum and instruction was meaningless if high school graduates could find no jobs in the community. She thought that economic development of the area was as important to reducing high school dropout rates as was the curriculum she was brought in to develop. She proposed doing a study of the job needs in the community and an inventory of community skills and potential businesses that might be generated by local people, and that a skilled community organizer be brought in to help build a development plan. Neither the leaders of the school district nor active parent groups felt that such activities were the responsibility of the schools, and the project never began.

EXAMPLE 1.2

DEFINING HEALTH PROBLEMS IN A PUERTO RICAN COMMUNITY

A Puerto Rican community agency in Hartford, Connecticut, was using census and survey data to support its advocacy efforts in the areas of housing, employment, and education on behalf of the Puerto Rican/Latino community in the region. A group of ethnographers from the University of Connecticut approached the organization to assess its interest in initiating a health research and development program. Agency staff, community leaders, educators, and researchers formed a committee, the Puerto Rican Health Committee, to identify health problems that required ethnographic research. One problem identified in new arrivals to local U.S. schools was schistosomiasis, a parasitic infection carried by snails and contracted through exposure to infected water. Children were becoming infected in Puerto Rico and expressing symptoms in local schools in the United States. An ethnographic study of schistosomiasis and other health problems, as well as strategies for seeking help about their health among newly arriving families, was conducted in a local middle school with a large Puerto Rican population that wished to develop a school health clinic. The study provided the scientific basis for justifying the creation of the clinic—which is now 15 years old—even though it confirmed that schistosomiasis was not an important health problem for Puerto Rican children in Hartford (Schensul & Schensul, 1978).

Key point   *The most important characteristics of applied ethno-graphic research, then, are the following:*

- Applied ethnographic research focuses on problems that are identified as important by both the researcher and key people in the setting where the research is to take place.
- Its results are useful to members of the community or institutional setting in solving the problem.

Ethnography as a Way to Create Theories of Culture

Key point   Unlike qualitative research in general, the principal and most important characteristic of ethnography is that it is rooted in the concept of culture. The end product of ethnography—the story or narrative—constitutes a theoretically informed interpretation of the culture of the community, group, or setting. *Ethnography generates or builds theories of cultures—or explanations of how people think, believe, and behave—that are situated in local time and space.* These theories or interpretations, specific to a particular context, can be tested by attempting to replicate the study in the same setting, although replication of ethnographies rarely is possible because subsequent studies necessarily take place at a different time, and the people, spaces, and context of the original study cannot be reassembled easily. Nevertheless, cultural theories generated in one ethnography provide the basis for hypotheses, hunches, observed patterns, or interpretations to be explored and developed in the same and other, similar settings.

CHARACTERISTICS OF ETHNOGRAPHY

The seven characteristics that mark a study as ethnographic are as follows:

- It is carried out in a natural setting, not in a laboratory.
- It involves intimate, face-to-face interaction with participants.
- It presents an accurate reflection of participants' perspectives and behaviors.
- It uses inductive, interactive, and recursive data collection
  and analytic strategies to build local cultural theories.
- It uses multiple data sources, including both quantitative
  and qualitative data.
- It frames all human behavior and belief within a sociopolitical and historical context.
- It uses the concept of culture as a lens through which to
  interpret results.

Ethnographic Studies Are Conducted on Natural Settings

Critical to the production of an ethnographic report or
story is the ethnographic process, or how the research is
conducted. The first defining characteristic of ethnography
as scientific inquiry is its commitment to producing a story
about events *as they occur in their natural settings*. Examples
of natural settings where people interact with one another
are playgrounds, classrooms, meetings, street corners, people's homes, clinic waiting rooms, courtrooms, shopping
malls, after-school programs for young people in community-based organizations, clubs and voluntary associations,
workplaces, basketball courts, and shooting galleries for
drug users.

Unlike experimenters, whose work we describe in the design section of this book, ethnographers generally do not manipulate or create the settings or situations in which responses to interventions are solicited, obtained, or measured. Some exceptions to this rule do exist, however, such as when ethnographers use group elicitation techniques or focused group interviews, which call for bringing respondents to a single location where the research will be conducted with them. In applied ethnography, researchers exert control when they incorporate research results into community-based controlled experimental designs that test alternative solutions to social problems. However, even in these situations, ethnographers prefer to create interventions that may be standardized but are conducted in natural field settings or with naturally occurring networks or groups of people.[1]

Cross Reference: See Book 1, Chapter 4, for more information on selecting research designs; Book 3, Chapter 2, for information on conducting focused group interviews; and Book 7, Chapter 1, for ways of integrating ethnography into programming

Ethnography Involves Intimate and Reciprocal Involvement With Community Members

Key point

A second hallmark of ethnography is that *ethnographers must become intimately involved with members of the community or participants in the natural settings where they do research. Intimate involvement means building trust between the researcher and the participants and often calls for a special kind of friendship.* In ethnographic research, gaining trust is sometimes referred to as **building rapport**. The process of building rapport differs depending on whether the researcher is an insider, or member of the group (with an already established role and relationships); an outsider (unknown to the group); or a partner (collaborator in the process of research and/or change). Trust is not built overnight—it takes time and considerable effort. It takes even

Definition: Building rapport requires the researcher to gain the trust of people involved in the research community

more time and effort when the researcher is perceived as different from the research community in such distinguishing features as gender, social class, culture, ethnicity, race, language, religion, caste, or role. The degree to which difference is perceived will vary depending on the target community, how much importance is given to any one of these features in the local setting, and the attitudes and behavior of the researcher. Researchers may delude themselves into thinking that trust is easily achieved, but this is far from the truth. They may be unaware of just how privileged or superior their status is vis-à-vis the people whom they study or how, as researchers, they are situated and perceived in a setting. Even the existence of long-term relationships cannot ensure that research participants will not withhold information, act out roles different from their normal behavior, distort information, or give socially acceptable responses to questions, thus biasing the data they provide to researchers. The techniques that ethnographers have developed for overcoming these barriers are summed up in the term *building rapport*. The process of building and maintaining rapport in the field is continuous—it does not end until the ethnographer leaves the research site.

The intimate relationships we have been describing generate for ethnographers a number of responsibilities that other researchers do not face to the same degree. As we will describe, many kinds of research, including surveys and experiments, require a degree of detachment or impersonality on the part of the researcher. By contrast, the research methods and data collection techniques chosen by ethnographers should foster and enhance intimacy between the researcher and the community in question, rather than maintain distance between them.

Ethnography also requires mutuality. Ethnographers develop close friendships in the research site that result in

Cross Reference: See Book 6 for a discussion of how these characteristics affect the ethnographer's work

Key point

expectations of reciprocity, help, assistance, and participation in the social life of the community. And if, as is often the case, researchers live in the same community as that in which the research is being conducted, they cannot avoid either being "in the field" at all times or the feeling of being "on call" if a research participant in the community of study needs something. Additionally, because applied ethnographers collect and analyze data on an ongoing basis, they are likely to be invited, and indeed expected, to provide feedback to people in the field and to participate in other development efforts, even in the early stages of the research process. Finally, for all researchers, but especially for those who live, work, and do research in their own community or who are committed to a particular direction for change, it is difficult to avoid meeting or working with people whose views stand in opposition to their own. These are issues described in greater detail in Book 6 on the role of the researcher.

Cross Reference: See Book 6 for guidance in building and maintaining relationships in the field

Emphasis on Participants' Perspectives and Meanings

Key point

/ *A third hallmark of ethnography is its commitment to accurate reflection of the views and perspectives of the participants in the research.* Ethnographic stories are built around and told in the words, views, explanations, and interpretations of the participants in the study. One of the most important reasons for building trust with members of the community is to ensure access to these views. When investigator and participant build a trusting relationship, together they create a safe and open environment in which the voices or opinions and views of the participants emerge in an authentic way. The traditional view of ethnography required the ethnographer to synthesize observations, interviews, written texts, and other data to produce a single story—an interpretation or theory of the culture in question. As communities or cultures changed, and as the practices of ethnographers changed with them, researchers began to recognize that communities could not be represented by a single perspective. The existence of different perspectives and behaviors—often referred to as multiple voices, polyvocality, or intragroup diversity—began to be recognized in ethnographic texts. Current practice makes it the responsibility of the ethnographer to ensure that all voices in the study are included in the text of the ethnography (Bernard, 1995; LeCompte, 1997; Marcus & Fischer, 1986; McLaughlin & Tierney, 1993; Pelto & Pelto, 1978; Weis & Fine, 1993).

During the 1970s and 1980s, social scientists across all the social science disciplines hotly debated whether or not researchers had the right to write up their ethnographic reports or stories as if they were a member of the group they were studying. Controversy raged even when researchers themselves *were* members of the group under discussion, and even if their writing conscientiously reflected diversity of behavior or perspective within the group. Many contemporary ethnographers now view their work to be a written interpretation of what multiple actors or spokespeople said and did in an ethnographic setting. These reports often leave the reader to arrive at his or her own interpretation of the culture.[2]

In applied ethnographic work, however, ethnographers are not only interpreters of words and deeds but participants or stakeholders in the uses of the research for problem solving. **Stakeholders** are people who have a vested interest in ensuring that the results of the research are used to solve the problem the research is addressing. They become spokespeople and interpreters along with the ethnographers, working hand in hand with the ethnographer to construct the social and political context of a problem, read

Definition:
Stakeholders are people who have a vested interest in what the research results are and how they are used

Cross Reference:
See Book 6, Chapter 2, on building research partnership

and interpret ethnographic data together, and define the best and most effective ways of using the results for community benefit. Some terms that have been used to refer to this general approach are *action research* (Schensul & Schensul, 1978; Stringer, 1996), *collaborative research* (Schensul & Stern, 1985; Stull & Schensul, 1987), or *participatory action research* (Whyte, 1991). *Rapid rural appraisal* is the term used by those researchers involved in agricultural and economic development (Scrimshaw & Gleason, 1992). Ways of constructing these research partnerships will be addressed in Book 6.

EXAMPLE 1.3   ➤•➤•➤

PARTNERSHIPS AND COLLABORATION ON A PROJECT
ON AIDS RISK AND DRUG USE IN ELDER ADULTS

Injection drug use is a major source of HIV infection in the cities of the northeastern United States. Ethnographers Jean Schensul and Kim Radda were interested in the potential for HIV infection among older adults. Working with a team that included health educators and staff and director of a regional area agency on aging, they pooled the ethnographic experience of AIDS educators working with older men, the concerns of older injection drug users and men addicted to cocaine, and the ethnographic data collected from older injection drug users and commercial sex workers. This resulted in a picture of risk behaviors and interactions among older men and women of diverse ethnic backgrounds in the Hartford area that all stakeholders could use in further research and health education efforts (Schensul, Radda, & Levy, 1999).

Use of Inductive, Interactive, and Recursive Processes

A fourth characteristic of ethnographic research is that *it uses inductive, interactive, and recursive processes to build theories to explain the behavior and beliefs under study.* In theory building, researchers start with both the research problem (or question) and a series of hunches, guesses, initial hypotheses, **models**, and concepts that they are interested in exploring and that relate to the research problem. These hunches or guesses are investigated in initial interviews and observations. They are then elaborated and retested through continued collection of data using the same or different methods—or both. The process continues until new information confirms a stable pattern, and the model appears to be complete. Glaser and Strauss (1967) refer to this process as "**grounded theory**." Spradley (1979) refers to the same process as domain and structural analysis, whereas LeCompte and Preissle (1993) and Merriman (1988) refer to it as recursive analysis. Recursivity refers to the cyclical nature of this kind of analysis; it moves back and forth between inductive analysis—which uses specific items to build more general explanatory statements—and deductive analysis—which applies general explanatory statements to groups of specific items (Schensul, 1998-1999). The result is what LeCompte (1990) terms a successive process of developing item, pattern, and constitutive or interpretive levels of analysis. The following example illustrates the use of recursive analyses to build a theory of AIDS risk among unmarried women industrial workers in Mauritius.

Key point with Definition: Inductive research aggregates specific and concrete data to create more general and abstract ideas about the composition of cultural scenes, social and physical phenomena, and explanations for why events occur as they do

Definition: Models are hypothesized relationships among concepts or domains of culture

Definition: Grounded theory or recursive analysis refers to the continuous interaction between data and hunches or hypotheses until a stable cultural pattern appears

Cross Reference: See Chapter 6 for an introduction to analyzing ethnographic data, and Books 2 and 5 for approaches to analysis of ethnographic data

EXAMPLE 1.4

BUILDING A THEORY ABOUT AIDS RISK IN MAURITIUS

In conducting ethnographic research on AIDS risk among unmarried young people in Mauritius, Steve and Jean Schensul worked with the head of the national family planning program, Geeta Oodit, to develop a conceptual framework. Initial interviews were focused on exploring changes in Mauritian family structure, peer relationships, and workplace dynamics that offered young men and women new opportunities to meet and be alone together, thus exposing them to more opportunities for sexually transmitted diseases and HIV infection. After interviewing Mauritian experts in each of these areas, Schensul, Schensul, and Oodit developed a taxonomy of subareas to explore, including family work patterns, family supervision, health of family members, peer activities, types of peer relationships, workplace status, workplace social life, workplace informal settings where men and women interact, and male-female relationships at work and in supervisory relationships. These subareas produced an initial set of concepts that formed the basis for semistructured interviews with a sample of 90 young women in three factories. The concepts then were reformulated and tested in a survey instrument used with another sample of 600 young women in factories. The final result was a conceptual model or theory of factors predicting HIV prevention knowledge and sex risk behaviors that could be tested out in a sexual health intervention program (Schensul, Schensul, & Oodit, 1994).

We do not want to suggest that ethnographic theory building uses inductive processes only. In fact, the recursive or iterative analytical process typical of ethnography uses both inductive and deductive processes to generate theoretical explanations. Ethnographers engage in bottom-up inductive thinking—that is, they generalize from concrete data to more abstract or general principles—by drawing from their data and experience in the site while simultaneously thinking deductively from the top down—that is, by applying more general or abstract ideas from theories that are relevant to their work to the concrete data they have collected. These theories often come from the work of other researchers.

At the same time, ethnographers also formulate on-site hunches and working hypotheses that serve as initial explanations for their data collection plans as they proceed. In the iterative or interactive process of constructing each piece of an explanatory theory, ethnographers can draw from theories of individual or group behavior; from theories of learning, development, social disorganization, perception, or self-efficacy; from structuralist, linguistic, postmodern, or feminist theories; or theories based on class, culture, social race, power, resistance, empowerment, or any other social science concept or theory available. Choice of theories depends on the personal preferences and disciplinary training of the research team and what appears to be appropriate to the problem or its solutions.

EXAMPLE 1.5

BUILDING A THEORY ABOUT TEACHER BURNOUT

Gary Dworkin, a sociologist, was dissatisfied with the theories that social scientists used to explain why teachers burned out and became alienated from their work. All the theories he found had been developed by psychologists. They located the source of burnout in individuals and posed as solutions either self-help schemes that advocated trying harder to adjust to difficult conditions, or stress reduction programs.

From the perspective of someone such as Dworkin, who is very familiar with the rigidities of public schools in the United States, these theories and the solutions they led to were not very satisfactory. Dworkin chose instead a sociological explanation (Seeman, 1975) for burnout based on "structural strain," or the idea that when societies and the institutions within them change too rapidly, individuals within the institutions find it impossible to cope. Dworkin found that teachers enter the profession as novices with expectations for how they should act and which behaviors yield success, and these expectations are based on what they were trained for and experienced as students themselves. However, on the job in contemporary schools, these old strategies do not work. Teachers feel that students are disrespectful, will not work, and cannot be punished. That sense that "the rules have all changed, and I cannot do anything about it," Dworkin says, causes teachers to lose faith in their abilities and in the institutions themselves. Instead of urging individual teachers to try harder to reduce their stress, Dworkin argues for structural changes in the reward systems and organization of schools—changes that help schools to better reflect the realities of current social conditions and therefore reduce teacher burnout (Dworkin, 1985, 1987).

Ethnography Uses Multiple Types of Data

Another characteristic of good ethnography is its *inclusion of both qualitative and quantitative data* (cf. Bernard, 1995; Pelto & Pelto, 1978). Ethnographers are data collection "omnivores" (Spindler & Spindler, 1992); that is, they make use of any and all types of data that could possibly help shed light on the answer to a research question. An ethnographic study always involves qualitative investigation. However, it may also include quantitative methods. Generally, ethnographers first conduct initial qualitative or exploratory research to find out what actually is happening in a particular scene. Only then do they decide which key variables and domains should be investigated quantitatively. These initial qualitative investigations provide data for the development of context-specific and relevant quantitative measures. Once this is done, quantitative measures can be used to verify qualitative findings and to improve generalizability of initial findings to the whole community.

Alternatively, ethnographers can choose relevant measures used by other researchers investigating the same economic, psychosocial, or cultural domains and adapt them for use in their own research site. For ethnographers, however, the aim is less to use standardized or nationally normed and validated measures (i.e., to favor reliability and generalizability) than it is to select or create measures that best match how research subjects understand the cultural domain in question (i.e., to favor validity).

Ethnography Examines Behavior and Belief in Context

The sixth hallmark of ethnography is that it views all elements under study as existing in a **context.** The term *context* is used to refer to the diverse elements—for example, people, groups, institutions, history, economic and political factors, features of the physical environment—that

Cross Reference: See Book 2, Chapter 8, on building ethnographically informed surveys

Cross Reference: See Book 2, Chapter 10, for a more complete discussion of reliability and validity in ethnographic research

Definition: Context refers to elements in a setting that influence the behaviors of individuals and groups

influence the behavior and beliefs of individuals. Context also refers to the cultural, historical, political, and social ties that connect individuals, organizations, or institutions. What individuals or organizations say, do, or believe can never be understood completely without understanding the social, political, cultural, economic kinship, and even personal matrices in which they are embedded, as Example 1.6 illustrates.

EXAMPLE 1.6

NAVAJO AND EUROPEAN AMERICAN DIFFERENCES
IN DEFINING A SCHOOL DISTRICT'S PROBLEMS

Westerners studying American Indian cultures often find that the explanations they give for events are quite different from—and often no less useful than—those given by local people. During a particularly bad year in the school district she studied on the Navajo Nation, Margaret LeCompte was told that the two deaths among faculty, a student suicide, the leaking roof in the new gymnasium, and a computer glitch that irrevocably erased two whole—and just finished—grant proposals so that they could not be submitted in time were all indicators that someone in the community had violated taboos and thereby created disharmony. LeCompte had more "rational" explanations: heart attacks, alcoholism, an incompetent contractor, and the failure of staff to plug computers into surge protectors during a thunderstorm. But none of LeCompte's explanations had the power to make things better. Navajo teachers suggested organizing a Blessing Way Ceremony to bring the school and its staff back into harmony with nature and the community. The superintendent of schools, a Navajo, volunteered to be the "patient" to be cured, thus representing the district itself. Following the ceremony, LeCompte noticed improved morale among the staff and a genuine hiatus in calamities (LeCompte & McLaughlin, 1994).

Another very different example shows how interpretation of research results is enriched by contextual/historical framing, and how the use of the research can be influenced by organizational and community responses.

EXAMPLE 1.7

THE CONVERGENCE OF GOOD RESEARCH, HISTORY, AND COMMUNITY
ACTIVISM TO IMPROVE SERVICE QUALITY FOR PUERTO RICAN WOMEN

In 1981, ethnographic survey research conducted by the Hispanic Health Council in Hartford, Connecticut on health- and mental health-seeking behavior in the Puerto Rican community included questions on reproductive health and contraceptive use. These questions were an organizational response to the then prevailing stereotype that Puerto Rican families included many children. When asked what their contraceptive of choice was, more than 50% of the sample of women interviewed responded "*l'operacion*" (sterilization). Many of the women who responded in this way were under the age of 40, still in their childbearing years, with only two or three children. Clearly, women were using sterilization as a form of contraception. Further ethnographic investigation revealed that Catholics and Protestants alike viewed sterilization as more acceptable than other forms of contraception in the eyes of the church. Other advantages for women were permanence, low cost relative to other methods, and convenience.

However, sterilization has a long and controversial history in Puerto Rico, and in light of this history, some members of the research team raised questions about the degree to which women were informed about the nature of the procedure and its permanence. Most of the local sterilizations were done at one hospital in close proximity to the community. When efforts were made to disseminate the results through a press conference, the press tried to convince researchers and community leaders to blame the local hospital directly instead of describing the more complicated situation portrayed by the research results.

At the same time, a group of community activitists that was familiar with the fertility control measures imposed upon Puerto Rican women in Puerto Rico in the 1950s decided independently to criticize the hospital for its lack of attention to informed consent, using public tools of confrontation that included picketing. The combination of careful and responsible research with community activism resulted in improved informed consent procedures, better reproductive health care at the hospital, and, eventually, close working relationships between the hospital and the community (Gonzalez, Schensul, Garcia, & Caro, 1982).

Ethnography Is Informed by the Concept of Culture

The seventh hallmark of ethnography is that its interpretation of what people say, do, and believe is guided by the concept of **culture**. Without an emphasis on culture, a study can have all of the six attributes listed in the definition and still not be an ethnography (Wolcott, 1987).

Definition: Culture consists of the beliefs, behaviors, norms, attitudes, social arrangements, and forms of expression that form a describable pattern in the lives of members of a community or institution

WHAT ETHNOGRAPHY IS

What, then, *is* ethnography? Quite literally, it means "writing about groups of people." More specifically, it means writing about the *culture* of groups of people. All humans and some animals are defined by the fact that they make, transmit, share, change, reject, and recreate cultural traits in a group. All ethnographers begin—and end—their work with a focus on these patterns and traits that, lumped together, constitute a people's culture. The result of such a focus is the document we call an ethnography.

Culture is not an individual trait. If what we observe is unique to an individual and is not repeated by others in similar settings, it is not culture. Although individuals *can* create cultural patterns by inventing them and communicating them with others, a cultural feature or element exists only when it is shared. By definition, culture consists of group patterns of behavior and beliefs which persist over time. Therefore, a group (even a small subgroup) must adopt a behavior or belief and practice it over time if it is to be defined as cultural rather than individual or personal. For example, the insertion by a handful of adolescents of safety pins in their earlobes could be viewed as a form of *personal* mutilation until the use of safety pins and other hardware as jewelry became commonplace in the punk subcultures of North America and Europe.

Culture also can be treated as a mental phenomenon, that is, as consisting in what people know, believe, think, understand, feel, or mean about what they do. Goodenough's (1956) definition of culture as what we need to know (not do) to function as a member of a society is illustrated in the following example.

EXAMPLE 1.8   ➡•➡•➡

USING CULTURAL INFORMATION TO SELECT APPROPRIATE RESEARCH INSTRUMENTS

R. Rhoades describes an innovative informal group interview technique for collecting quantitative data on potato production in Nepal without using questionnaires. His research team found that questionnaires were not a good way of obtaining data from Nepalese farmers about the use of potato varieties. Farmers found the questionnaires unfriendly and were not interested in them. Members of the research team then decided to go to the market, where they bought every available type of potato they could find. Local farmers added to the pool of potatoes. Researchers then proceeded through the potato area, stopping at each village and demonstrating their collection of potatoes. Farmers gathered round; began to share information; and discussed characteristics of each variety, arranging them in local categories of appreciation, zone production, disease resistance, culinary quality, and place in the meal. Researchers were able to use these dimensions of discussion to obtain quantitative data for each variety of potato, noting that "the quality of these data was much higher than with a questionnaire using categories that were outside a farmer's reality" (Rhoades, 1992, p. 67).

Cross Reference: Rhoades's potato sorting activity is similar to the pilesort elicitation technique described by Borgatti in Book 4

➡•➡•➡

Culture also can be treated behaviorally in terms of what people *actually* do (as observed) as opposed to what they *say* they do (as reported), or as "norms" (the expected) versus "practices" (the actual). Evelyn Jacob (1987) summarizes the differences between these two approaches with the terms "patterns *for* behavior" and "patterns *of* behavior." Patterns *of* behavior represent behavioral variations or choices in the group; patterns *for* behavior represent cultural expectations for behavior.

EXAMPLE 1.9

DISTINGUISHING PATTERNS *OF* BEHAVIOR FROM PATTERNS *FOR* BEHAVIOR

Ways of greeting people are strongly patterned by culture. Cultural patterns *for* behavior dictate that in North American society, individuals meeting one another feel that they must extend their right hands to shake hands firmly in greeting. This pattern is so firmly ingrained as denoting cordiality that people feel compelled to apologize if their right hand is injured so that they must shake with their left hand or not shake at all. Patterns *of* behavior—based on observation—indicate that there are many variations in greeting patterns. Whereas professional women usually always shake hands, in informal settings, women often do not shake hands at all, or do so rather limply. They may hug or kiss someone in greeting instead. Children almost never shake hands unless prompted by adults, and many foreigners, immigrants, and indigenous American Indians do so only uneasily because their own cultures either mandate other forms of greeting or, in fact, have mandates about *not* touching strangers.

Both the behavioral and cognitive/emotive aspects of culture occur within economic and political contexts that are marked by distinctive social arrangements, or ways in which people relate to one another in institutions. Thus, culture also includes the social arrangements and institutions within which people interact, or that are designed to meet their instrumental or emotional needs.

Although we have defined culture as shared patterns of meaning and behavior, we do not want to imply that everyone in a cultural or social group believes the same things or behaves in the same way. In every group and in any domain of culture we could imagine, substantial variation will exist. For example, peoples' attitudes, beliefs, and behaviors will vary depending on their ethnicity, racial identity, gender, gender identity, birth order, social class and status, educational level, age, place of residence, time of immigration, and other factors considered relevant in the social and political rhetoric and composition of contemporary life. Unique historical events, environments, spaces, and places also can induce variation in the behavior or beliefs of individuals or subgroups. It is critical to consider these variations when engaging in ethnographic research in order to avoid cultural stereotypes and ensure that all of the many voices contending in a setting are heard.

A Note on Ethnicity, National Identity, Culture, and Race

One mistake often made by researchers and laypeople alike is to confuse culture with ethnicity and ethnicity with national census categories. By **ethnicity**, we mean self-identification in a sociopolitical grouping that has both recognized public identity and a conservationist/activist orientation. We often mistake ethnicity for those categories used to define sociopolitically important groups in national censuses. For example, the U.S. census includes five contrived ethnic groupings: Hispanics, Asian Pacific Islanders, Native Americans, Blacks, and Whites. These designations create many problems. For example, they combine and confuse social definitions of race (white, black) with national origin (Anglo, African American, or Arab American). The terms lump together people and groups that have nothing in common except a label (Americans of Spanish, Cuban, Mexican, and Chilean origin). Because they are not based in social, historical, biological, or cultural realities, they have no social meaning to people clustered under these contrived headings.

A further problem is that "mixed" ethnic heritage is not taken into consideration when such broad designations are

Definition: Ethnicity refers to self-designated membership in a group working toward maintaining its cultural and political presence in a national system applied. There are increasing numbers of individuals who self-identify or who are forcibly identified as members of one group when their parents and/or grandparents were members of two or more racial/ethnic groups. Among these groups are African Americans in the United States, who once were defined legally and historically as "Black" if one of their great-grandparents was Black—regardless of the individual's skin color or facial features. American Indians still are recognized as Indian by the federal government and by many tribal governments if one great-grandparent was recognized to be Indian, even if the contemporary individual has never been involved in American Indian cultural practices. Many people in this position now are agitating to become recognized as "mixed" and want to have their multiple origins specified.

Such broad designations may be useful conventions in quantitative and survey research, but they are not useful in ethnographic research except when

- They hold meaning for research participants.
- They affect research participants directly through public policies, programs, or attitudes.
- They affect the relationship between the researcher and the research community.

Even in quantitative research, census designations are too broad and diffuse to predict strongly anything other than sociodemographic characteristics such as income, education, and occupation, which are all indicators of socioeconomic status.

Ethnicity is a term usually applied to those groups working to maintain their cultural and political identity and to ensure protection, advancement, and access to resources for their members in a national system. Members of an ethnic group usually, although not always, consist of people of the same national origin. For example, Haitians, Irish Ameri-

cans, and Italian Americans each come from a single, identifiable country. West Indians may refer to themselves as
West Indian, West Indian/Caribbean (regional designations), or as from their island nations of origin (e.g., Bar-
bados, Jamaica, or Trinidad).

Ethnic affiliation is a choice that often brings with it
Key point responsibility for behaving in particular ways. *Thus, not all*
people of similar national origin will identify themselves as
members of the same ethnic group. For example, not all
people of Mexican origin in the United States define themselves as Chicanos—a term that denotes a particular kind
of political activism. Similarly, some people of African origin living in the United States might not choose to refer to
themselves as African American.

Because ethnicity is created in response to particular
Definition: situations, but does not always involve shared culture,
Intra-ethnic members of an ethnic group may vary in how they think or
variation refers act. There may be considerable **intra-ethnic variation** even
to differences in within a self-defined ethnic group. *It is very important to*
beliefs and behaviors *identify and explore such variation in order to avoid stereo-*
of members of a *typing, and also to make sure that programs and policies*
specific ethnic group *geared toward enhancing the position of designated ethnic*

 Key point *groups respond to the multiplicity of identities, voices, needs,*
and interests in the group.

The Impact of Cultural Politics
on Identity and Research

Some of these identities have had a profound effect not
only on how people define who they are and how they—and
others—should behave, but also in how research should be
carried out and data should be interpreted. As conscious-
ness of past and contemporary oppression grows among
marginalized or subordinated groups, members of these
groups argue against traditional labels; power relationships;

and ways of thinking, knowing, and interacting. Such reactions began as colonized people and subordinated minority groups became aware of how they have been portrayed in research studies, especially ethnographies. Non-European researchers such as Edward Said (1978, 1994), Trinh Minh-ha (1989), C. Mohanty (1988), Gyatri Spivak (1988), and others have criticized the romanticized depictions of so-called primitive or exotic peoples and the tendency of European and North American researchers to interpret non-Western cultures in terms of Western European concepts. *One of the strengths of ethnography is that the methods used* **Key point** *produce a picture of cultures and social groups from the perspectives of their members.* Ethnographies tell the story of a group from the group's perspective as much as from the ethnographer's point of view.

Postmodern, feminist, and critical theorists have helped to clarify the existence of such Eurocentric presentations. Feminist theory has exposed the dichotomous—male versus female—nature of traditional scientific theory, research methods, and interpretations and has demonstrated how it has tended to privilege male perspectives. African American and Latino/a feminists (note mixed designations) have argued that traditional feminism developed from middle-class white female experience and ignores the ways of thinking and knowing of women who are non-white or poor. To accommodate notions of class, race, and culture as well as power, these researchers have turned toward qualitative and ethnographic approaches to research and based their research on critical and constructivist theories that legitimate **Cross** social criticism and negotiated meaning. Combining ap- **Reference:** proaches in this way permits the multiple voices of diverse See Chapter 3 communities of women to engage in an inclusive dialogue in this volume in which meanings are shared and debated, conflicts can for an explanation arise and be resolved, and new ways of addressing changes of these theories in policy and practice can occur.

The next chapter addresses the circumstances under which ethnographic research is the best approach to research in problem-oriented settings.

NOTES

1. For more information on ethnographically informed interventions in field settings, readers are referred to Chambers (1987), Van Willigen (1993), Schensul and Eddy (1985), and *Practicing Anthropology,* a journal of the Society for Applied Anthropology.

2. The noted anthropologist Clifford Geertz's book *Works and Lives* (1989-1990) discusses the pitfalls of this approach, as does LeCompte's 1997 chapter in the *International Encyclopedia of the Sociology of Education,* "Trends in Qualitative Research Methods," and Singer's (1990) article in *Current Anthropology.*

2 ━●━●━●━

WHEN AND WHERE IS ETHNOGRAPHY USED?

*Conditions
Calling for
Ethnographic
Research*
•
*Which Settings
Are Most
Appropriate for
Ethnographic
Research?*

Ethnographic research methods are not appropriate for all investigations. The conditions we described in Chapter 1 provide some clues as to when ethnographic approaches are likely to be most useful. In this chapter, we spell out details of appropriate times to use ethnographic research.

CONDITIONS CALLING FOR ETHNOGRAPHIC RESEARCH

Ethnography should be used to:

- define the problem when the problem is not clear
- define the problem when it is complex and embedded in multiple systems or sectors
- identify participants when the participants, sectors, or stakeholders are not yet known or identified
- clarify the range of settings where the problem or situation is occurring at times when the settings are not fully identified, known, or understood
- explore the factors associated with the problem in order to understand and address them, or to identify them when they are not known
- document a process

29

- describe unexpected or unanticipated outcomes
- design measures that match the characteristics of the target population, clients, or community participants when existing measures are not a good fit
- answer questions that cannot be addressed with other methods or approaches
- ease the access of clients to the research process and products

Clearly, the decision to use ethnographic design is strongly influenced by the characteristics of the research population, the conditions of the research setting, what the researchers need to know, and who the research partners are. Below, we list some examples of issues that could best be studied using an ethnographic approach to research. The following story demonstrates the value of ethnography when the problem is not clear.

EXAMPLE 2.1

USING ETHNOGRAPHY WHEN THE PROBLEM IS NOT
CLEAR: CONFLICT IN URBAN COMMUNITY GARDENS

A park system in a large urban area has provided land for a community gardening program. In some parks, the program has functioned without provoking or producing disagreements among users or complaints from other park users or neighbors. In other parks, the opposite is true. The conflictual situations vary from one park to another: users of gardens and parks differ; locations differ; the communities surrounding the park are different; and in some instances, newly arriving ethnic groups are displacing long-term residents—and garden users—in a community. Finally, the kinds of situations that provoke conflict appear to vary. The community gardens administrator does not know why conflict exists in some of the gardening sites, or how to organize an infrastructure to oversee the transition of management to local users. She would like to reduce conflict, ensure continuing use of the gardens, and transfer management of the gardens to local community groups.

The next example illustrates the uses of ethnography when the problem is clear but its causes are not well understood.

EXAMPLE 2.2

USING ETHNOGRAPHY WHEN THE ORIGIN OF THE PROBLEM IS NOT
WELL UNDERSTOOD: PNEUMONIA AND CHILD MORTALITY IN CHINA

Pneumonia is the most frequent cause of death in children under the age of 3 in China. National and provincial medical personnel would like to develop cost-effective programs to decrease the mortality rate. Some professionals attribute the high death rates to poor medical care; others to mothers' negligence; still others to an increasing income gap between rich and poor people and overall increasing levels of poverty. The Ministry of Health would like to introduce a national program to reduce the death toll from pneumonia. Until more is known about the circumstances in which pneumonia deaths occur, introducing such a program is likely to be less than efficacious.

The next situation shows how ethnography can be useful in defining a problem. In this example, the problem appears to be late school enrollment, which is a problem for school administrators but not necessarily for parents. Research could be used to discover why the late enrollment is so common. Here, multiple perspectives on the problem, and finding out what the real problem is, are challenges for ethnographic research.

EXAMPLE 2.3

USING ETHNOGRAPHY TO DEFINE A PROBLEM:
PUERTO RICAN SCHOOL ENROLLMENT IN THE UNITED STATES

Administrators in an urban northeastern school system of the United States discover that more than 70% of all the children who were eligible for enrollment in the district at the end of June have failed to enroll for the following year. More than 60% of elementary-age schoolchildren in this district are Puerto Rican. Some educators blame the enrollment problems on Puerto Rican parents, attributing the very low rate of reenrollment to the fact that Puerto Rican families leave early for Puerto Rico before the enrollment period begins. They assert that a campaign to "educate" Puerto Rican parents about the importance of early enrollment and entrance to the fall school program must be implemented. Other educators argue that the reasons for late enrollment or return are not known and must be identified before any program of improvement begins.

In each of these situations, debate exists over both what the actual problem is and its potential causes. The debates raise questions of power, gender, race and ethnicity, context, personal need, and other factors influencing equitable access to information and resources. These debates cannot be resolved without additional information, but prior research has not yet been carried out to shed light on the context and likely causes of the problems and their potential solutions. The service providers or practitioners who identified the problems in the first place recognize that more information would be helpful. But they also see that the survey methods ubiquitous in applied social science research are not likely to help them very much because they do not know enough yet to develop a survey instrument. They cannot say with certainty what would be included in a survey instrument, who should be asked to fill it out, and what sample size would be appropriate.

The questions posed by the problems just described are intended to lead to program or policy changes. They are not intended to test or evaluate alternative programs or interventions that call for an experimental design. Narrative research in these instances could provide personal accounts or testimony that would reveal the multiple perspectives needed to elucidate the problem. Furthermore, the problems are complex. They do not lend themselves to single explanations or solutions. Fixing them—finding a way to do something about them—requires a variety of different approaches, perspectives, and methods. Also needed is the participation of the various parties or stakeholders. Without such participation, remediation is not likely to be successful nor to endure over time. Building stakeholder involvement or participation, however, requires that researchers understand the culture of various stakeholder groups—that is, become familiar with their beliefs, perceptions, values, philosophies, communication style, and be-

Cross Reference: See Book 6, Chapter 2, on building research partnerships

haviors—and negotiate with them. These processes are readily embedded in the conduct of ethnographic research.

Yet another reason why ethnographic research is preferable to survey or other approaches to research in the above situations is that ethnography emphasizes discovery; it does not assume answers. Ethnography uses open-ended methods that allow investigators and others to gather information identifying the source of the problem, rather than simply assuming that it is known from the start. The fact that ethnography is almost by definition participatory also facilitates investigation in situations like those illustrated above. The ethnographer's unique relationship with key individuals in the study site, such as service providers, teachers, and community leaders, brings all of these individuals into the research process and calls upon them to offer important insights—which constitute data for the ethnographer—to help clarify the situation.

Ethnography also helps people learn what they need to know to develop either survey research or plans of action as precursors for things like educational programs, intervention strategies, or recommendations for policy change. Participants in the examples we have described know too little about the research site, the population, or the problem to begin their research with survey or other quantitative or numerical methods of data collection. For example, all of the participants who might be affected by the particular problem have not yet been fully identified, nor have the ways in which they might be affected been defined. The causes of conflict, gaps in communication, or problems accessing educational and other resources have not yet been well clarified. Although the practitioners might have sought traditional explanations arrived at through ordinary means—that is, by soliciting opinions of experts and professionals—past efforts to use such experts have not always proven useful. Finally, because cultural practices, beliefs, attitudes, and histories of constituent groups in the setting can affect each situation, these must be documented and their intersections and mutual influences explored before solutions can be created. For all of these reasons, we believe that ethnography is the best approach in the above examples.

Our next example describes a situation in which ethnographers actually have instruments to "measure" individual behavior quantitatively, based on self-reports from research participants, but exactly what happens in the field may be more complicated than what can be determined by responses on those instruments.

EXAMPLE 2.4

USING ETHNOGRAPHY WHEN STANDARD INSTRUMENTS CANNOT ACCESS
THE WHOLE STORY: WHY AIDS PREVENTION STRATEGIES SOMETIMES FAIL

HIV infection often is transmitted through the exchange of infected blood via injection drug use. The AIDS virus enters the body when drugs are injected with dirty or infected needles and syringes. The infection can be passed from person to person when needles are shared without sterilizing or bleaching them first. Bleach kills the AIDS virus. Thus, injection drug users who avoid sharing their needles or clean their "works" with bleach prevent infection in both themselves and others. Two ways to help prevent the spread of AIDS are to make sure that injection drug users have clean supplies of needles so that they do not have to share them, and to make sure that they have plenty of bleach to clean their needles, syringes, and other paraphernalia that they use to heat and dissolve their drugs before injecting. Injection drug users report that they obtain clean needles regularly from the local Needle Exchange Program, and that they also get and use bleach "most of the time" to clean their works. But while doing an ethnography of drug users, Philippe Bourgeois observed them doing these things only some of the time; when they were in a rush and did not have a clean needle handy, they would use a used needle. Furthermore, not every member of a group of drug users used the bleach kit. Sometimes, drug users used the same bleach a number of times, assuming that this was safe (Bourgeois, 1996). Thus, in this instance, observations from the field qualify or even disconfirm what people report as survey responses.

◆━◆•◆━◆•◆━◆

Data such as these can be obtained only through ethnographic field research and are of central importance in designing culturally framed interventions that actually work. Such data provide critical information about the people, the circumstances, the constraints of the setting, and the resources needed to make a positive difference in people's behavior.

WHICH SETTINGS ARE MOST APPROPRIATE FOR ETHNOGRAPHIC RESEARCH?

Ethnographic research can be conducted in almost any setting, depending on the question and the preferences of the researcher. Most ethnographic researchers are concerned with social issues and problems. Many of their research questions have to do with problems in the relationship of community residents, families, or "clients" to the institutions—educational, health, cultural, or political—that are supposed to serve them. Thus, there has been a strong tradition of ethnographic research in local communities and in the interaction between these communities and service agencies, housing programs, educational institutions, hospitals and clinics, and other service sites. This research has been used to identify cultural, political, and structural factors that

- impede community development
- make the implementation of appropriate educational, health, or other services more difficult
- create obstacles to the prevention of known risk factors for various diseases or social problems
- limit public artistic, linguistic, or cultural expression

EXAMPLE 2.5

USING ETHNOGRAPHY TO IDENTIFY OBSTACLES
TO DIABETES CONTROL AMONG PUERTO RICANS

Diabetes is known to be a significant problem among Latinos in general. In Hartford, Connecticut, preliminary research showed that Type II diabetes is much more common among Puerto Rican adults than among adults of other ethnic groups. Because research is showing that exercise and diet in childhood can influence the onset of diabetes and cardiovascular disease in adults, a team of ethnographers and epidemiologists responded by conducting a study of activities and energy outputs in Puerto Rican children. The 1-year pilot study took place in Hartford and New Haven, Connecticut, and resulted in a set of assessment tools that can be used to measure children's activity outputs. The researchers were surprised to find that the results of measuring energy outputs showed that boys were expending four times more energy than were girls for the same time period. These results, combined with ethnographic observations and in-depth interviews with mothers, showed how different cultural expectations for behavior of boys and girls, coupled with structural barriers to sports and other activities in school and in the community, resulted in reduced activity levels for girls (Schensul, Diaz, & Woolley, 1996).

The results of ethnographic work such as that described above can be helpful in shaping community-based programs and educational strategies that can bring about changes in personal, family, and community structures and behaviors.

Ethnographic researchers also work with staffs of schools and higher education institutions, health clinics and hospitals, arts and environmental organizations, and programs serving children and youth. The following example illustrates how one professional used ethnography to define her role in a state arts agency.

EXAMPLE 2.6

USING ETHNOGRAPHY FOR COMMUNITY ARTS PROGRAMMING

Most states in the United States have an official State Folk Arts Program initiated with funding from the National Endowment for the Arts and following NEA guidelines for folk arts and public programming. Anthropologist Winnie Lambrecht has many years of experience in heritage/folk arts and filmmaking. For the past decade, she has worked in a variety of capacities with the Rhode Island Arts Council, conducting field research that undergirded the exhibits and other public programs on the heritage and folk arts of cultural groups that she mounted within the state and in New England. In addition, as a filmmaker, she uses film as a medium for communicating community culture to the public.

Increasingly, federal bureaucracies are recognizing the value of ethnographic research and researchers. They are hiring anthropologists and other social scientists to initiate intramural ethnographic research and fieldwork in organizations as diverse as fisheries, agencies dedicated to cultural preservation, schools setting up multiethnic curricula, and community-based environmental protection and planning efforts.

EXAMPLE 2.7

USING ETHNOGRAPHY IN ENVIRONMENTAL
PLANNING, PROTECTION, AND DEVELOPMENT

The Environmental Protection Agency's (EPA) Bureau of Community Based Environmental Planning (CBEP) is dedicated to comprehensive community involvement in environmental planning and development. This process requires facilitators who understand community dynamics and have a background in environmental sciences and social sciences. Recognizing the value of applied ethnography in this process, the CBEP inquired as to whether the Society for Applied Anthropology, an international professional association of applied social scientists, wished to develop a cooperative agreement with the EPA. An important component of this agreement was the recruitment and involvement of qualified ethnographers with group facilitation and community development experience in technical assistance and training for community-based environmental planning in communities around the country. The Society for Applied Anthropology submitted an application for a 5-year cooperative agreement. Significant components of the agreement are the production of position/review papers and public education symposia, regional and national internships, and field support for local projects (Society for Applied Anthropology, 1996).

Summary

In previous sections, we have emphasized that ethnographic research is scientific—it is rigorous, systematic, repeatable, and logical. At the same time, the ethnographic approach to research offers investigators the opportunity and the tools necessary to enter into new field situations and to investigate newly identified social issues or behaviors without the constraints of preexisting instruments or assumptions about the situation. Furthermore, ethnography requires an understanding of what research participants' behaviors mean to *them* rather than imposing potentially irrelevant interpretations on those behaviors.

SUMMARY OF USES OF ETHNOGRAPHY

- To better understand a problem
- To illustrate what is happening in a program
- To complement quantitative data on program process or outcomes
- To complement and better explain survey data
- To identify new trends

Ethnography has many different and important uses. It can be used to arrive at a better understanding of a situation or a problem. It can also be used once a program is in place to document and understand better what is happening in that program, and to provide information on program staff and participants that can complement other, quantitative data collected on the program. Ethnography can be used throughout the life of a program, to complement a survey, or to explain quantitative results or outcomes, especially those outcomes that are unanticipated or unexpected. Finally, ethnography is very useful in the identification of new trends (e.g., changes in drug use patterns or changes in the attitudes of parents toward the use of new curriculum materials in schools), new solutions for social problems, and potential problems in the implementation of new policies, such as the effects of welfare or social service reform on communities. Because these questions are generic—that is, they apply across many different settings, agencies, and types of problems—ethnography has appeal for a broad range of users.

3 ━●━●━●━

PARADIGMS FOR THINKING ABOUT ETHNOGRAPHIC RESEARCH

WHAT ARE RESEARCH PARADIGMS?

All research is informed by particular worldviews or perspectives held by the researcher and scholars within his or her discipline. These perspectives are called **paradigms.** A paradigm constitutes a way of looking at the world; interpreting what is seen; and deciding which of the things seen by researchers are real, valid, and important to document. The most common paradigms in social science research and evaluation are positivism (the oldest); critical theory; interpretive, phenomenological, or constructivist theory; ecological theory; and social network theory. Many researchers make use of each of these approaches, depending on their research questions, their own personal preferences, and the constraints and needs of the research setting. Sometimes, an ethnographer's perspective on culture—how he or she thinks and writes about culture and with whom—is situated in a synthesis of several paradigms. In the pages that follow, we will review the way in which people understand culture in the context of each of these approaches. We will

Definition: ☀
A paradigm is
framework for
interpretation or
a way of viewing
the world

41

also consider the position likely to be taken by researchers as they consider

- The types of questions they wish to ask
- The cultural and social domains important in the research
- The communities they plan to study
- How and with whom the process of interpretation of data is likely to occur
- How and with whom uses of research results are likely to be negotiated

THE POSITIVISTIC PARADIGM

Positivistic research represents an effort to duplicate the rules and assumptions of the biological sciences in the social sciences. It has been an especially important influence in experimental psychology, medicine, mental health, education, clinical studies, and the growing domain of prevention research. The positivist approach argues that reality is observable and understandable, and that if the research is conducted with a properly representative sample of participants, the findings that a researcher obtains are true or probably true for everyone in the study site—that is, they can be generalized to the study population as a whole.

Cross Reference: See Chapter 4 of this book for ways in which positivist research designs are used in ethnography, and see Book 6 for a stereotypical portrait of the traditional positivist researcher

The aim of positivistic research is explanation leading to prediction of causal relationships. For example, researchers interested in whether or not medical interventions or innovative educational programs are effective would think as a positivist does and set up an experiment or quasi-experiment to test the relationship between the intervention and what the experimenters think (or hope) its outcome will be.

Positivistic research methods can be both qualitative and quantitative. In both cases, positivists assume a distinct conceptual and social separation between the researcher's influence and the object or events being studied. This is what is meant by the term **objectivity** in positivist research. In practice, objectivity requires the researcher to withhold his or her own biases and prejudices about the research and the people involved in it and to try to control any outside influences (including his or her own hopes about the outcomes) on the research results. The researcher tries to avoid influencing or "manipulating" the setting as much as possible, even when the data are generated through face-to-face interaction in the field site. In Chapter 4 of this book, you will find a more extended discussion of experimentation that, along with the use of standardized survey instruments and some kinds of field observations, is informed by positivistic principles that enforce the separation or detachment between the researcher and the study respondents or other subject matter.

Positivists believe that the research methods they use can and should be neutral and value free, although they understand that the researchers' own values play a role in the selection of the research question. They also realize that values or priorities influence how research results are used. But positivist researchers themselves feel that they should remain disinterested in the actual conduct and outcomes of the research—at least for the duration of the project—so that their own strong interests or passionate commitments cannot become a source of bias in the conduct of the study or the interpretation of the results. They are also committed to using research methods and techniques that maintain this objectivity.

Because they believe that control of researcher biases is, for the most part, a matter of both technical rigor or finesse and researcher self-discipline, positivists tend to believe that class, social race, ethnicity, gender, age, individual and group history, or other characteristics of the researcher should not influence the hypothetical causal models that drive or initiate a research project without theoretical jus-

Definition: Objectivity in research involves establishing control over researcher bias and outside influences by creating a conceptual separation between the influence of the researcher and the people or events under study

tification. This does not mean that there cannot be a match between the views and priorities of the researcher and the researched, or that these variables should not be included in the development of research models. It does require that the priorities and personal interests of the researcher alone must not influence the actual execution of the study and (especially) the interpretation of research results.

Positivists may become quite active as advocates for or with the people or problems they study once the research project is complete. However, positivists would seldom, if ever, get involved in discussing research results with participants or introducing or conducting any nonresearch-related programs or interventions in the research site while the actual research is under way—especially if they believed that such activity would influence the outcome of the research. If the researcher were to intervene in the setting, it would violate positivist requirements that researchers maintain an affective neutrality with regard to study outcomes and the researcher's own influence on conduct of the investigation. One important exception to this position is experimental research design, where the point of the research is to evaluate the impact of an intervention or experimental program. Here, the research project calls for the investigator/researcher to guide the conduct of the program so that it can be evaluated rigorously by the research team. In such instances, the researchers would avoid exercising direct influence on the evaluation, during both the program and the evaluation.

To the extent that they do collaborate with nonresearchers on a project, positivists discuss the conduct of their studies with research partners—those nonresearcher/ collaborators joining in the design and execution of research projects. Such partners, who can include institutional administrators, heads of community organizations and institutions, and directors of funding agencies, can play a variety of roles in the research and can even modify or change the selection of research methods and techniques. These partners may participate in interpreting the results, often offering new and interesting perspectives on the data that the researchers might not have considered. They can also contribute in important ways to interpretations of unexpected or unpredicted results. Elicitation of insights from research partners is a form of **member-checking** that ensures the validity, authenticity, and credibility of results.

Member-checking is not the main way that positivists disseminate research results to research participants. This is because the first audience for the positivist's research results is usually the scientific community. Positivists have a deep commitment to furthering science, and they consider it unprofessional, if not unethical, not to share important results with the scientific community. Sharing of results with other audiences —including the participants of the research—certainly is important but is carried out in addition to scientific publications. Applied ethnographers, however, give priority to dissemination to research participants.

Definition: Member-checking involves corroborating information elicited from one research participant with information from other members of the same group

Cross Reference: See Book 2, Chapter 10, for a discussion of validity and reliability in ethnographic

THE CRITICAL PARADIGM

Critical theorists are interested in how the history and political economy of a nation, state, or other system exerts direct or indirect domination over the political, economic, social, and cultural expressions of citizens or residents, including minority groups. Critical theory guides investigation into the sources and dimensions of inequality in such systems. In the critical paradigm, scientists are expected to function as intellectual advocates and activists. Researchers are expected to use the tools of research to discover inequities and to find ways—whether through research, dialogue, intervention, political action, or policy change—to bring about change in inequitable distributions of power, cultural assets, and other resources.

Critical theorists, like positivists, believe that researchers can capture reality accurately in the specific historical and geographical contexts they study. However, they also assume that the interpretation of the cultural products (words and text, norms, behaviors, symbols, physical objects, etc.) they examine is influenced by the context in which they are produced and reproduced. Because critical theorists view cultural behavior and beliefs as situated within a specific historical era, they believe that these behaviors and beliefs can change over time. They also note that much of what may appear to be cultural practice among oppressed people is a response to their subordinate status. In the United States, for example, many educators believe that the poor hygiene and unhealthful eating habits of many low-income children represent cultural preferences when, in fact, they are the result of inadequate plumbing or water supplies and insufficient family income to purchase nutritious meals.

For some critical theorists, capitalist institutions and their cultural products are targets for research that identifies flaws in their structure and promotes their abolition. Other critical theorists define restrictive or inequitable structures and cultural institutions more broadly, arguing that research and transformation can be planned and carried out in any restrictive setting in both incremental and large-scale ways. In other words, they believe that institutions can be transformed, and they seek ways of using research to serve the transformation process. Action research, which brings participants into the research and reflection process, is one such approach to change, although it is not always informed by the critical paradigm.

Critical theory calls for a focus on the ways in which gender, class, culture, race, ethnicity, and power intersect to shape inequities. Included in this focus is the requirement that researchers themselves be aware of how their own class status; racial, ethnic, and gender orientation; and power relationships vis-à-vis research participants affect what and how phenomena are studied and how data are interpreted.

Because the final aim of critical research is to call attention to the inequitable actions and policies of the dominant social paradigm or institution and to engage in selected activities or actions—guided by the findings of critical research—in order to bring about change, the critical approach requires congruence among the aims, objectives, and values of the researcher and those of the group(s) involved in the study. To bring about such congruence, all participants, including researchers, should be involved in the research process, because the research is intended to be empowering—that is, to demonstrate how and in what ways participants are in positions of subordination or domination (or, in some cases, both), and how they can act to change both their own situation and that of others. Values play an important role in the critical paradigm and should be identified and shared early in the negotiation of the research process. Critical theory also asks researchers to assist in enhancing research participants' individual and group potential for accessing important social and economic resources, for entering the political arena, for engaging in self-expression, and for becoming activists in shaping their own futures.

Although critical theorists, like positivists—or any researchers, for that matter—are bound by ethical considerations to do no harm to research participants, they may be caught in a dilemma when their commitments to the well-being of the oppressed conflict with the interests of the groups or people acting as oppressors. Both may be participants in the research, but the latter may consider their interests to be in peril if the former act in ways designed to improve their situation or reduce the degree to which they are oppressed. The researcher's dilemma in such cases is that he or she must choose among the following:

- Decide which side to favor
- Attempt to promote a dialogue by means of the research project or during review of research results
- Strategize ways to do the most good—or the least harm—for all

Cross Reference: Book 6 provides a discussion of the researcher's role and ways of conceptualizing and building partnerships that include consideration of inequities and how to address them

THE INTERPRETIVE, PHENOMENOLOGICAL, OR CONSTRUCTIVIST PARADIGM

Interpretivists, phenomenologists, and constructivists all base their approach on a cognitive or mentalist view of reality. Although the terms are often used interchangeably, and in fact mean quite similar things, they do have their origins in different disciplines. The term *phenomenology* comes from philosophy. *Constructivism* comes from and is used most by educational researchers, sociologists, and psychologists, and *interpretivism* or *interactionism* tends to be used by sociologists and anthropologists. In this book, we will use the term *interpretive* to refer to all three.

Crucial to interpretivists, constructivists, and phenomenologists is the "social construction of reality." This means that, unlike positivists—who assume that reality has some tangible referent and that agreement can be achieved on its nature given sufficient time and careful research—interpretivists believe that what people know and believe to be true about the world is constructed—or made up—as people interact with one another over time in specific social settings. This conceptualization is similar to Jacobs's notion of "patterns *for* behavior," which we cited earlier. Unlike the positivists, for whom research results are "true" at least in a probabilistic sense and are empirically verifiable, these theorists believe that the social "constructions of individuals and groups are not more or less 'true' in an absolute sense, but simply more or less informed and/or sophisticated" (Lincoln & Guba, 1985, p. 111; see also Berger & Luckmann, 1967). Furthermore, constructs are not fixed or immutable; they can be altered through dialogue or over time, and the alterations can lead to new constructions or views of reality and new ways of acting (cf. Nastasi & DeZolt, 1994). A distinction between interpretive and positivistic approaches is that the former are inherently relativistic because they assume that all constructs are equally valid and important.

Interpretivists view culture as both cognitive and affective, as reflected in shared meanings and as expressed in common language, symbols, and other modes of communication. They believe that culture is created in a process as many individuals share or negotiate multiple and overlapping socially based interpretations of what they do and what occurs in local situations. Culture, then, is an abstract "construct" put together or "constructed" as people interact with each other and participate in shared activities.

Another key component to the interpretive paradigm is that it always defines shared constructs and meanings as "situated"; that is, they are located in or affected by the social, political, cultural, economic, ethnic, age, gender, and other contextual characteristics of those who espouse them. These characteristics influence how individuals think, believe, and present themselves. An important element in the interpretive position, then, is first to define the sociopolitical status of each speaker or participant before his or her place in the web of meaning is articulated by the researcher. Unlike positivists or critical theorists, interpretivists stick close to local meanings and find it difficult to tell only one "story." Instead, they tend to present complex accounts as polyvocal texts, or stories told in the voices of many different people or constituencies.

Interpretive, constructivist, and phenomenological approaches are inherently participatory because meaning can be created only through interaction. For researchers, this means that they must participate in the lives of research participants in order to observe social dialogue and interaction—the process of creating constructs, ideas, and meanings—as it occurs. Furthermore, authentic or valid individual constructs or ideas can be elicited and refined only through interaction between and among all researchers, participants, and partners in the project. In this sense, the data and findings of interpretivists are created and recreated as the research proceeds. Important to interpretive researchers is that the constructs or meaning systems of researchers, participants, and research partners all carry equal weight, because negotiated meaning cannot occur unless the researcher is a full participant in the process. The nature of this interaction blurs the distinction between researcher and researched, subject and object, bringing all parties together as equal partners in the process of generating and interpreting data. Such blurring would never be permitted in a positivistic research project.

Interpretivists believe that
cultural beliefs and meanings are

- socially constructed
- situated, and therefore relative to a specific context
- not fixed
- negotiated
- multiply-voiced
- participatory

Interpretive approaches are not activist oriented by definition. Thus, unlike critical theorists, interpretivists do not necessarily begin with, nor are they expected to produce, results that commit to action, even though many scholar activists/applied ethnographers do enter the research dialogue with change-oriented positions that then come to be negotiated. Under such conditions, the consensus that results from interactions in the research site can produce a deep sense of shared understanding of a particular social

problem as well as a set of shared norms that leads to specific directions for action (cf. Nastasi & DeZolt, 1994).

EXAMPLE 3.1

CONSTRUCTING SHARED NORMS ABOUT ASSESSMENT AND
EVALUATION IN AN ARTS EDUCATION PROGRAM

One feature that interested Margaret LeCompte during her work with a middle school arts program was how the teachers used portfolios to assess the students' progress, especially when the portfolios produced by students in visual arts, literary arts, theater, and instrumental music differed considerably. However, because she knew that the teachers had not had time during the initial stages of the program to work on assessment procedures, LeCompte did not want to embarrass the teachers by asking them directly for their grading criteria—which she knew probably had not been clearly articulated. Unbeknownst to LeCompte, however, the teachers were very concerned that they be consistent in their assessment procedures across the arts programs, but they did not know how to go about establishing common criteria for grading. During a staff meeting, this concern was aired by the Visual Arts teacher. When LeCompte and her assistants suggested to the teachers that they could use ethnographic interviews to elicit from them their respective criteria, and then use data from the interviews to develop a set of preliminary criteria to use as the basis for discussion, the teachers were delighted. They did not have the time to hold such a discussion themselves, and if LeCompte's interviews could generate a preliminary common rubric, they could then do the final polishing themselves. In this way, LeCompte was able to collect data on assessment procedures, and the teachers were able to do a better job of consistent grading.

THE ECOLOGICAL PARADIGM

The ecological paradigm has a long history in ethnographic research stemming from the early sociologist Emile Durkheim and the early 20th-century work of structural anthropologists such as A. R. Radcliffe Brown and Bronislaw Malinowski. Researchers working with the ecological paradigm:

- view individuals as functioning in a social context that influences their behaviors. Context consists of the human and physical environment in which events take place; it includes social levels (e.g., family groups, peer networks, school or work settings, community, and the wider society) and sectors (e.g., social, technical, and environmental).

- see these levels, institutions, or sectors within a community as systematically related to and affecting one another.

- believe that change should be introduced in all levels or sectors simultaneously.

- think that research that is guided by the ecological paradigm should identify those contextual elements with the greatest influence on individual or institutional behavior. Unlike the critical theorists, however, ecologists have few preconceived notions about which of these elements is most important.

Definition: Environment refers to any contextual feature: social, cultural, institutional, political, or geophysical

Ecologically oriented research looks for continuous accommodation among individuals, institutions, and the **environment** (Poggie, DeWalt, & Dressler, 1992; McElroy & Townsend, 1979). In both research and results, ecologists emphasize adaptation rather than conflict, and they seek to understand how social systems persist and adapt to conflict as well as how they change. For ecologists, the direction of change emerges from localized research—it is locally specific because the perspective guides researchers to explore interactions in local settings. The primary difference between critical theorists and ecologically oriented theorists is that concepts of class, power, and equity guide the former but not necessarily the latter. Thus, for the former, directions of change are implicit from the beginning, whereas for the latter, they emerge inductively from the research itself.

THE EMERGING SOCIAL NETWORK PARADIGM

More properly termed an emerging paradigm than a paradigm in its own right, social network perspectives provide an important analytic framework for social science research. The study of social networks has constituted an important component of the sociologist's work for many years. In anthropology, kinship networks and genealogies have been more salient. Recently, social network research has been integrated across disciplines, causing social scientists to define a new paradigm in social science research—the network paradigm. This new integration combines the work of a number of people:

Cross Reference: See Book 4 for a discussion of social network research

- Theorists, who are concerned with the diffusion of innovations through social systems
- Communications specialists, who are concerned about the flow and exchange of information in communities, societies, and worldwide
- Resource specialists and community planners, who are interested in the ways in which community organizations relate to one another to serve clients
- Epidemiologists, who are concerned with the transmission of communicable diseases through interpersonal networks
- Prevention researchers and program specialists, who want to intervene with natural groups or become more effective in disseminating information about disease prevention through social systems

A network perspective offers a view of a community or other social setting that is very different from the view that sees the community as composed of essentially unrelated individuals. The study of social networks allows social scientists to situate individuals within their families, among their peers, and in relation to representatives of other social or cultural institutions. Investigating social networks also provides social scientists with the opportunity to observe and document important exchanges between and among individuals, explore the locations where these exchanges happen, and determine what other factors might influence them. The concept of "social network" need not apply to individuals only. It can also apply to communities that are linked together through exchanges of people, resources, and infrastructures, or to organizations connected by users, boards of directors, or other factors. Understanding what the relationships and associations are among these institutions can provide important information about how communities or larger systems work.

The social network paradigm has evolved over the past 40 years (Galaskiewicz & Wasserman, 1993; Johnson, 1994; Wasserman & Faust, 1993). Historically, network theory has been used in studies of family systems and adaptation (Bott, 1957; Cross, 1990); in diffusion studies concerned with the flow of innovation, information, or infection in populations (Trotter, Rothenberg, & Coyle, 1995); and in studies testing the efficacy of group interventions in natural groups or networks (Nastasi et al., in press; Schensul & Berg, 1997; Schensul et al., 1996; Trotter et al., 1995).

Cross Reference: See Book 4, Chapter 1, for more information on methods of social network research

Social network researchers are interested in natural groupings defined ethnographically or descriptively through observations in the field. They are also concerned with personal or ego-centered networks, which are defined in terms of individuals who are related to a single respondent. Some researchers concentrate on personal or ego- centered networks; others are interested in broader community networks, termed "full relational networks," where each individual is considered in relation to all the others in the group.

Some researchers wish to understand only the way social networks work. Others are more interested in what might influence the development of particular types of social networks, such as whether age, ethnicity, or both are related to size and composition of drug-using networks. They may choose to investigate whether or not specific types of networks, defined by composition, size, density, or specific behaviors (e.g., drug use or vegetarianism) are associated with other behaviors or conditions, such as unprotected sex or cardiovascular conditioning. Social network researchers conduct research with social networks in several different ways:

- Through ethnographic mapping or description (Trotter, Bowen, Baldwin, & Price, 1996; Trotter, Bowen, & Potter, 1995)

- Through survey techniques in which a random sample of respondents is asked to list its contacts or close associates and to indicate what these contacts do in relation to the research topic, ego-centered network surveys (Trotter, Baldwin, & Bowen, 1995; Trotter & Schensul, 1998)

- Through "snowball" or network sampling, in which respondents list their contacts, and all or a random sample of contacts are interviewed to find out about their relationships with the respondents and with others. Eventually, almost everyone in a community is interviewed (McGrady et al., 1995; Needle, Coyle, Genser, & Trotter, 1995; Trotter, Bowen, Potter, & Jiron, 1994).

Network research is one important component in an ecological approach and can be incorporated readily into the work of all others described in this chapter.

A PARADIGMATIC SYNTHESIS

We believe that all of these approaches to research are important. In our own work, we draw upon all of them in each research situation. The positivist approach is helpful in reminding us that concepts, instruments, and methods that have been developed, standardized, structured, and normed can be useful in any research setting. The methodological principles embodied in probabilistic survey research force us to identify and consider the importance of variation in study populations. The tenets of experimental design are helpful in responding to research partners' needs for demonstrating outcomes—or whether or not a program "works"—even when the limitations of these outcomes are apparent. Computer software for coding, managing, and analyzing qualitative or text data offers much better opportunities now for establishing and maintaining interrater reliability and making it readily possible to engage in repeat analyses. Systematic data collection tech-

Cross Reference: For more information on systematic data collection and elicitation techniques, see Book 3, Chapter 3

niques based on prior ethnographic elicitation and data collection strategies can be quantified into categorical variables or matrixes for quantitative analyses designed to demonstrate cultural consensus or patterning. These are all useful methods regardless of which conceptual approach is favored by the ethnographic researcher.

Critical approaches are consistent with our view that applied ethnographers should enter a study situation with the view that they will be expected to be instrumental in implementing change. At the same time, most important social science research nowadays is expected to consider the important dimensions of difference and such potential predictors of inequity as socioeconomic status/class, age, gender, social race, ethnicity, and ability. Most applied ethnographers discover local responses to national or even international situations once they are in the field. These responses generally involve difficulties that local residents have with interethnic or intercultural communication, or problems that communities face in lacking access to valuable resources as a consequence of income, gender, social/racial characteristics, or other "differences." The critical approach reminds us of the influence of global systems on local settings; views of "difference," for example, may be influenced by international media, and local inequities may stem from international economic policies and practices that influence local markets and local employment.

Like the critical approach, the ecological paradigm reinforces the idea that individuals do not function alone. Instead, they are embedded in formal and informal groups —the family, peer group, schools, community organizations—and are affected in many obvious and less obvious ways by community, state, national, and global dynamics. Power is only one of a number of important factors that influence individual and group behavior. One advantage of the ecological approach is that it directs attention to individual and group interaction with the natural environment and demands recognition of the effects of landscape, location, natural resources, climate, and environmental depletion on human behavior and interaction.

Finally, the emerging social network paradigm calls for considering social entities (individuals, families, organizations, and communities) as engaged in important exchanges with one another. The network paradigm forces us to recognize that none of these social entities can be seen as functioning alone. Instead, each is linked to and affects the others in ways that can be discovered. This frame of reference has implications for sampling and for data analysis. The implications are most significant for data analysis because the quantitative or numerical units that are the building blocks of network research are connected. Thus, the assumption that units are independent of one another and have an equally likely chance of being selected is not valid. Neither the principles that underlie random sampling nor the assumptions of quantitative data analysis that units of analysis are independent apply to network analysis. Its worldview that defines everything as linked, as well as its procedures for identifying, selecting, and "counting" or analyzing units, is distinct from other paradigms.

Regardless of who they are, ethnographers are likely to be situated differently in relation to their research partners, collaborators, or clients. It is possible, even probable, that they will have more education, income, status, prestige, and privilege than those with whom they work. To build trust between researchers and research participants, and to increase the potential for obtaining good information, ethnographers must always remember who they are and where they come from. While trying to establish common ground with respondents, they must also be aware of difference and how their perceived identity may influence the flow of communication in the field setting. Doing so requires reflecting on personal values and beliefs about who one is as well as why, where, and on what it is appropriate to conduct research, and how one plans to use research results. It is also necessary to be prepared to share personal plans and views without imposing them on others.

Applied ethnographic research also benefits greatly from an interpretive or constructivist viewpoint—its emphasis on the generation of shared meanings and its recognition of the importance of local context and cultures in human behavior and beliefs. Interpretivism provides a strong rationale for collaboration in research; it is through establishment of research partnerships that generation of the best and most relevant questions, instruments, interpretations, and use can be ensured. To benefit from collaboration with the study community, researchers must negotiate with partners in each of these domains. It is especially important for researchers and their community partners to negotiate the interpretation and meaning of research results when the results of data analysis do not clearly point to directions for action, or when they are counterintuitive or different from what was expected. In such cases, all partners must use both their knowledge of the setting and any new information to discuss and agree on results and how to best use them. Table 3.1 compares and summarizes the concerns, foci, procedures, processes, and goals of each of the five paradigms discussed above, as well as describes the differing roles each dictates for researchers and participants in research studies.

Summary

The specific frame of reference or paradigm underpinning the research process is important to the overall structure of the ethnographic study. It is especially important in determining the goals of the research and how—and by whom—data will be interpreted and put to use. Once the researcher is aware of these issues—and it is the task of the project director to make all parties involved in the project cognizant of them—it is time to begin the process of structuring the research itself.

TABLE 3.1: A Comparison of Paradigms

	POSITIVISTIC APPROACHES	INTERPRETIVE APPROACHES	CRITICAL APPROACHES	ECOLOGICAL APPROACHES	NETWORK APPROACHES
CONCERN	Self as defined by society/form/social structure, i.e., what's going on outside individuals	Society/form/social structure as defined by self, i.e., what's going on within and between individuals	Self as defined by the structure of domination, i.e., what's going on within and between individuals as a consequence of their given material and historical conditions	Self as defined by social structures representing levels of influence: i.e., what's going on within individuals influenced by family, peers, school, work, community and society	Self as defined by interaction with significant others in specific cultural domains: i.e., what's going on within and between individuals as a consequence of social relationships.
ORIGINS OF KNOWLEDGE	By definition, by deduction from laws or theoretical statements, from experience	From shared understandings, negotiation, histcrical and social context	From differential access to knowledge regarding historical context, political, economic, and social conditions	From beliefs and behaviors of individuals to knowledge of structural factors influencing their behaviors	From beliefs and behaviors of individuals to knowledge about their social interactions with important others
ROLE OF RESEARCHER	Affectively neutral, uninfluenced in the conduct of study by personal experience of the research	Involved, informed by researcher's personal experience in interaction with the study participants.	Educative, analytic, tranformative; active teacher/learner	Detached, uninfluenced in the conduct of study by personal experience of the research	Involved, informed by researcher's personal experience in interaction with the study participants; may also be detached and uninfluenced.
ROLE OF RESEARCHED	Affectively neutral, objective	Involved, subjective	Educative, analytic, tranformative; active teacher/learner	Detached, objective	May be either involved or detached; Objective or subjective.
FOCUS	Observable behavior. Measurement and quantification. Qualitative operationalization of variables. Controlling variance and bias.	Elicited meanings for observational behavior. Intersubjective understanding. Explaining variance and bias.	Structural asymmetries, critical consciousness, hidden meanings and assumptions, patterns of oppression. Exposing variance and bias.	Observable behavior and elicited meanings in relation to structures, policies, norms, behaviors typical of other levels in the system.	Observable and measured behavior, both qualitative and quantitative and elicited meanings in relation to explication of social relationships.

(continued)

TABLE 3.1: Continued

	POSITIVISTIC APPROACHES	INTERPRETIVE APPROACHES	CRITICAL APPROACHES	ECOLOGICAL APPROACHES	NETWORK APPROACHES
PROCEDURES	Definition (by researcher); Description (by researcher); Classification/ codification (by researcher); Enumeration; Correlation; Verification; Prediction	Definition (by subject); Description (by subject); Classification/codification (by researcher subject to member checks); Enumeration; Correlation/ association; Interpretation (by researcher in conjunction with subject); Communication	Definition (by researcher and subject); Description (by researcher and subject); Classification/codification (by researcher subject to member/checks); Enumeration; Correlation/ association; Interpretation (researcher in conjunction with subject); Communication (by researcher); Action/transformation (researcher and subject)	Definition (by researcher); Description (by researcher); Classification/codification (by researcher possibly subject to member/checks); Enumeration; Correlation/ association; Interpretation (researcher in conjunction with subject); Communication (by researcher); Verification; prediction	Definition (by researcher); Description (by researcher); Classification/codification (by researcher possibly subject to member/checks); Enumeration; Correlation/ association; Interpretation (researcher in conjunction with subject); Communication (by researcher); Verification; prediction
PROCESS	Achieving control of behavior by modeling its study after procedures used by scientists studying the physical universe	Achieving understanding of behavior by analysis of social interaction, meaning, and communication	Achieving change in structure and behavior by exposing hidden patterns of meaning, communication, and control	Achieving change in structure and behavior by analysis of levels and their interaction	Achieving change in structure and behavior by identifying influence of interaction among members of a social group on one another.
GOALS	1) Generalization of results to subsequent similar events and phenomena 2) Development of universal laws which govern human behavior in all settings	1) Comparison of results to similar and dissimilar processes and phenomena 2) Development of workable and shared understandings regarding regularities in human behavior in specific settings	1) Analysis of results to unmask inequities in processes and phenomena 2) Development of emancipatory stance toward determinants of human behavior	1. Analysis of results to identify relationships across levels in a local situation. 2. Development of local predictors influencing individual, group and social behaviors. 3. Inductive development of regional and larger patterns and laws	1. Analysis of results to identify social relationships among related individuals; 2. Development of predictors of social influences on individual behavior 3. Generalization from local to universal rules

4 ━●━●━●━

AN OVERVIEW OF RESEARCH DESIGN

WHAT IS RESEARCH DESIGN?

Every systematic activity undertaken by human beings needs a plan of action. In research, the formal plan of action for a project is called a **research design**. Research designs are to researchers as road maps are to vacationers or blueprints are to architects and contractors; they tell the investigator how to proceed. However, they include much more information than two-dimensional maps or blueprints. A better analogy might be the detailed schedules and lists sent to clients by a very good travel company in response to the clients' concept of the trip they wish to take, and their questions about how to proceed—including not only maps, but a set of assumptions about what the travelers want to do, time lines, descriptions of destinations, where they will stay, what activities are planned, who they can expect to meet, anticipated meals, the equipment they need to bring, the types of people who will be on the trip, and, most important, what the trip will cost if planned in that way. Without such information, travelers are likely to end up in uncomfortable hotels, lacking proper clothing or equipment, without insect repellent, taking photographs of wild animals at the local zoo instead of in the forest. They may

Definition:
A research
design is a detailed
set of questions,
hunches, and
procedures, and
a plan of action for
the conduct of a
research project

61

have forgotten what they wanted to see, do, and learn in the first place; they might even run out of money.

PLANNING A RESEARCH DESIGN
AS A BLUEPRINT FOR ACTION

A good research design, like a good vacation plan, saves time, money, and headaches, and it permits the anticipated objectives of the activity to be achieved. The converse also is true. Therefore, it is wise to spend plenty of time at the beginning of the project planning and designing it—even though the time might not seem worthwhile initially. If the researcher is working as part of a collaborative team or with partner organizations, planning is not only more critical, but even more time-consuming. Planning with partners requires hammering out in advance shared ideas, responsibilities, and meanings as well as agreements regarding how to proceed. This includes deciding on the following:

Cross Reference:
See Chapter 3, this volume, for a discussion of research paradigms

- Which paradigms to use
- What the core research questions are
- Which methodological alternatives and approaches to data collection are best for the project

Regardless of the amiability of partnerships in the initial stages of research projects, the press of time and work inevitably uncovers unforeseen differences in perspective, work styles, and value systems as the project unfolds. Intercepting and preventing some of these at the beginning of the project can avoid unpleasant surprises.

Research Design as a Decision-Making Process

Researchers can choose from among many research design alternatives. Decisions about the choice of design are guided primarily by three main factors:

- The questions the investigator is trying to answer
- The resources (time, trained personnel, and money) he or she has at hand
- The characteristics, including the constraints, of the research site or setting

The initial tasks involved in creating a research design (or methodology) are the following:

- Framing the initial research question
- Building a conceptual starting point, preliminary theory, and hypotheses or hunches
- Identifying characteristics of an appropriate population to study and locating that population
- Finding and obtaining access to an appropriate research site
- Identifying and establishing relationships with relevant research partners.

These issues constitute the initial areas of concern in developing a research design. Once they have been addressed, researchers can then proceed to more technical considerations, such as how to do the following:

- Develop a data collection plan
- Design appropriate data collection methods
- Establish analytic procedures
- Develop ways of protecting the identity of research participants and the confidentiality of the information they provide, and for treating them ethically
- Establish guidelines and procedures for interpretation dissemination and utilization of research results

Each of these steps should be carefully considered, outlined, and described in detail in the initial research proposal, even if the work in the field calls for changes to be made (see Figure 4.1). Consideration of these steps has the advantage of avoiding conflict over research directions that we men-

(1)	(2)	(3)
Develop the Research Base	Decide on Research Methods	**Decide on Field Situation**
Frame questions	Determine sampling	Develop human subjects
Build guiding theory	procedures	guidelines
Identify population	Develop data collection plan	Determine staffing plan
Find research site	Design data collection	Define training protocols
Identify partners	methods and schedule	Determine field security
	data collection	

(4)	(5)
Select Data Analysis Procedures	**Determine Procedures for Dissemination**
Decide on text coding	Determine audiences
system	Decide on guidelines for
Decide on computerization	audienceinvolvement in
Decide on use of software	interpretation of data
for analyzing elicitation	Select dissemination settings
mapping or network data	and timel ines
Decide on procedures for	Determine dissemination
analysis of survey data	formats
Conceptualize triangulation	Predict resistance in advance

Figure 4.1. Steps in the research process.

tioned earlier. It also allows researchers to think through and prepare in advance for the problems that inevitably occur in the field.

The question of which design is best for the given research question is the first factor to be addressed. If the investigator wants to determine how a representative sample of people from a particular community feels about a problem or issue, a survey research design might be called for. Survey research usually follows certain principles of probability sampling, instrumentation, data analysis, and presentation designed to ensure that the results of the survey can be generalized to the entire population. If the researcher wants to know if Program A is more effective than Program B, then a controlled experiment is most desirable. The conventions of experimental design call for random assignment of subjects or larger units of intervention; pre- and posttesting; and "experimental integrity," or control over the conditions of the experiment.

On the other hand, if the researcher really does not know the characteristics of the population of interest, the parameters of the problem to be addressed, what should be included in a program, or even what its outcome should be, then ethnography probably is the most suitable choice. The conventions of ethnographic design call for exploratory investigation (participant observation and open-ended interviewing, described in Book 2); selective investigation of targeted topics (semistructured observations and interviews, described in Book 2); collection of data on cultural domains (described in Books 2 and 3); and generalizable survey data on individuals and networks (described in Books 2 and 4).

Of course, many projects require the use of mixed designs, where an initial design calling for a self-reported survey, for example, might be modified to include systematic observation. Or an experiment might require ethnographic research to help to describe, explain, and verify what is actually happening during the implementation phase. Finally, once exploratory ethnographic research has been completed, the final stages of ethnographic research often call for surveys based on random sampling of the study population in order to determine the distribution of specific behaviors or beliefs in that population. The challenge to the researcher is to choose the best combination of approaches for studying the research problem. In some cases, as the following example illustrates, the original approach to data collection must be modified or complemented to produce useful results.

EXAMPLE 4.1

USING ETHNOGRAPHY TO STUDY NONLOSING WEIGHT-LOSS CLIENTS

A group of weight-loss therapists collected data on their overweight clients by having them keep daily logs of what and how much they ate. The therapists could not figure out why their clients, whose daily self-reports of food consumption contained only approved low-calorie items, did not lose weight. They began to suspect that some of the clients were cheating. To check, they added a data collection strategy called "shadowing" for some of the clients, observing and taking notes on how they prepared their meals, what they ate, and how often. They found that clients did not exactly cheat, but they systematically served themselves larger portions than allowed, unable to believe just how small a 3-ounce serving of meat is. They also forgot to record small snacks and "tastes" that they consumed while preparing meals. The unreported increments almost doubled their allowable consumption of daily calories.

The self-reports were a very economical way to collect data. However, as the example above indicates, self-reports were not accurate. The original research design needed to be modified to accommodate the new data collection technique, the question that called for its use, and the analysis and integration of the new and different forms of data to be collected. The change also had an effect on the overall cost and duration of the project. This example demonstrates how a seemingly small change in sampling or data collection procedures can influence the entire research design or methodology planned for the project.

All of the design features mentioned in the first part of this chapter (from identifying the question to analyzing and preparing the data for dissemination) must be figured out in the context of logistical constraints. The most elegant research design in the world will not work if the researcher does not have enough money, time, or trained staff to carry it out. Thus, researchers always must keep in mind the need to assess the resources needed to conduct the research. The final considerations then, are the following:

- Deciding how—and whether—to sample from the population as a means of reducing the size of the group one must study
- Identifying logistical problems and solving them
- Locating, hiring, and training staff
- Determining as much as possible in advance the procedures for analyzing data, including use of computerized data management approaches to data analysis

The lists above make clear that designing a research project involves more than just choice of data collection techniques. We believe that research design really involves making a series of choices among alternative ways to proceed from start to finish in a research project. In the following pages, we discuss the variety of approaches to research available to social science researchers, outlining the strengths and limitations of each. Each approach has implications for the selection of study site, sampling, methods of data collection and analysis, cost, and duration. In Chapters 6 and 7, we discuss design considerations in greater detail, including sampling, data collection, and analysis.

The Range of Research Designs Used in Social Science Research

To aid the reader in choosing the right design, we provide Tables 4.1 and 4.2 (quantitative designs) and 4.3 (qualitative designs), which summarize the most common research designs used in the social sciences and their purposes. We include quantitative as well as qualitative designs because both can be used in the conduct of ethnographic research. We will begin with the quantitative end of the design continuum because readers may be more familiar with research plans involving the collection of quantitative data. Then, we will describe qualitative designs most frequently used by ethnographers and other qualitative researchers. Later in the chapter, in Tables 4.4 and 4.5, we will show readers how to integrate qualitative and quantitative research in each of

TABLE 4.1 Standard Survey and Experimental Research Designs Used in the Social Sciences

Design Type	Minimal Conditions of Use
Cross-sectional research: Population and sample surveys	— Clearly known problem and context — Previous identification of relevant domains or possible responses — A target population whose characteristics have been identified — Enumerated members listed by name or other discrete identifier
Experiments	— An hypothesis or prediction about the expected results of an experiment or controlled effort to induce change — Creation of a control or comparison group through random assignment of units — Rigorous control over conditions of treatment or implementation
Controlled field studies/ quasi-experiments and case-control studies	— A field setting interested in the problem — Treatment and comparison groups whose subjects' characteristics have been matched or clearly defined to indicate salient differences between them — An hypothesis or prediction about the expected results of an intervention — Rigorous control over conditions of implementation

the designs. Good ethnographers know when to choose one design over another and when to combine designs in their field research.

QUANTITATIVE SURVEY AND EXPERIMENTAL DESIGNS

Table 4.1 depicts the most common quantitative and experimental designs used in the social sciences and the conditions required for their use.

Cross-Sectional Research: Population and Sample Surveys

Surveys are the most widely used form of systematic data collection. One cannot read a newspaper, conduct a political campaign, institute a marketing strategy, or engage in public policy planning without encountering the results of surveys. They are used in the needs assessments that precede program planning and implementation for a specific group of people; in attitudinal surveys, which attempt to measure changes in attitudes or opinions; and in ethnographic projects to confirm the statements of key informants. Whether conducted by mail, telephone, electronic mail, or in person, surveys are used in any study in which the researchers need to elicit a limited amount of information from a large population whose characteristics—including the language they use, their age, location, and other demographic factors, as well as their accessibility and willingness to answer questions—already are reasonably well known.

Population surveys involve asking questions of an entire group of people; where populations are very large and resources preclude surveying everyone, sample surveys are used instead. Sample surveys involve using statistical procedures to draw from a large population a smaller group—or sample—whose characteristics are quite close to those of the larger group. Data collected from the smaller group are assumed to characterize what would have been collected from the larger group.

Cross Reference: See Fowler and Mangione, 1990, and S. Schensul in Book 2 for further information on the statistical procedures used to create systematic or random samples

The term *survey* can be confusing, because a survey is both a research design and a method of collecting data. A study that uses statistical methods to select respondents systematically or randomly and that has a survey instrument (an interview or a questionnaire) as its only source of data is said to use a survey design. However, survey instruments can be and often are incorporated into other kinds of studies, including ethnographies.

Although surveys can be quite efficient and economical, there are real limitations to their utility and validity.[1] They should only be used when:

- The population itself and the kinds of questions to be asked are already known
- The researchers are familiar with both the language and the vocabulary of the participants
- Researchers know whether the concepts and ideas used in the study are meaningful to the participants

Below, we describe several examples to illustrate how incomplete knowledge about the study population can result in biased or inaccurate survey results.

EXAMPLE 4.2

BIAS IN CENSUS SURVEYS

The U.S. Bureau of the Census traditionally bases its decennial headcount on members selected from household units. Despite attempts to define the term "household" as broadly as possible, certain segments of the population, including those who are homeless, go un- or undercounted because they cannot be located in standard living units.

EXAMPLE 4.3

BIAS IN TELEPHONE SURVEYS

U.S. political pollsters in 1948 seriously underestimated the strength of Harry Truman's support. Basing their estimates on a telephone poll, they predicted Dewey's victory, not realizing that the large number of people who did not have telephones, and who therefore were not polled, would vote overwhelmingly for Truman.

EXAMPLE 4.4

BIAS IN THE LANGUAGE OF SURVEYS

A team of researchers was constructing an interview to be administered to store owners about their attitudes toward what appeared to be an increasing incidence of petty theft, loitering, and panhandling at the local mall. One set of questions addressed the behavior of people under the age of 20. The researchers were surprised that even among themselves, they could not agree on a name for such individuals that did not have some kind of negative connotation. One researcher objected to the use of the term *juvenile*. "*My* kid isn't a juvenile; he's never been arrested." Another asserted that only when juveniles were delinquent did the term *juvenile* have a negative meaning. Others felt that *teenager* and *adolescent* also were unacceptable because they implied irresponsible or negative behavior. They compromised by using the term *young people*, explaining to survey respondents that they meant "people between the ages of 12 and 20."

EXAMPLE 4.5

BIAS INTRODUCED BY SURVEY INTERVIEWERS

Anthropologist Rosalie Wax (1971) reported how she helped sociologist David Reisman make sense of the responses of working-class women in the United States to his survey of attitudes toward participation in the political system. Reisman wanted to know if feelings of intimidation inhibited the participation of women with little education or status in civic life. Because he got very few answers to his questions, and because his respondents giggled or were silent when interviewers tried to probe further, he assumed that the women he interviewed either had little or no knowledge about political processes or had extremely limited communicative capabilities. Wax, whose background was similar to that of many women in the target population, simply went out and organized informal conversations with the women about politicians, elections, and the act of voting. One question that Reisman had asked provoked great derision among respondents: "That interviewer, he asked me if I ever felt afraid when I walked into a voting booth! Whatever in the world could make me afraid of a *voting booth*?? Of course I'm not afraid, but how do you answer a question like that?"

The examples above illustrate how crucial it is that the researchers be familiar with the behavior patterns and characteristics of the population to be surveyed—as in the first two examples—and agree among themselves about the terminology to be used—as in the last two. Even more crucial is that the language and patterns of speech in the survey be couched in the same meaning system and frame of reference used by the people who are to answer the questions. When surveys lack such **construct validity**, survey results become nearly useless, as was the case in Reisman's initial study of working class women, described in Example 4.5.

Definition: Construct validity refers to the match between the meaning intended by the researcher and the meaning assumed by the respondent

A limitation of surveys is that by themselves, they assess only what people think or know at a specific time—and for this reason, they are called **cross-sectional studies**, because they cut across and examine a particular section of events excised from the flow of time. Some researchers try to

Definition: Cross-sectional studies examine phenomena at a single point in time

correct for this limitation by using longitudinal designs that involve repeated interviewing at standardized intervals. Survey researchers call these *trend* or *panel studies.*

Definition:
Trend studies
interview cross-
sectional samples of
the same population
over time to
discern trends

Trend studies administer repeated surveys at specified intervals to different samples selected from the same population as the first one; their utility is limited somewhat because the samples selected for each subsequent interview contain different individuals from the initial set of respondents. Random selection at each point helps but does not fully eliminate bias in the selection of each group because the overall population may well have changed over time. **Panel designs** correct for this problem by selecting a large sample and then administering repeated interviews only to members of the original sample. However, the composition of the panel—and, consequently, the kinds of results obtained from it—can change significantly as members drop out over time. This may mean that the results obtained at the beginning of a study come from quite a different group than do those obtained at the end of the study. This can render the results somewhat questionable. Therefore, all panel designs must report on potential biases that derive from loss of respondents.

Definition:
Panel designs
interview the same
people at different
points in time to
discern changes
in the population

Surveys cannot provide much historical or contextual data to illuminate why people responded as they did. It is also difficult to corroborate the accuracy of survey respondents' answers if no other data are collected. However, combined with other forms of data collection, such as field observations, analysis of documents and artifacts, and informal conversations, surveys can add great strength to a study because they are the primary way that researchers determine whether or not ideas held and behaviors engaged in by a few people studied intensively are more widespread in the general population. They also can be used to determine the range of variation within a target population.

Experiments

Natural scientists, medical personnel, psychologists, educational researchers, evaluators, and funding agencies tend to be quite familiar with experimental and quasi-experimental designs. These are the primary designs used in these fields, in which research questions focus on determining whether an intervention or treatment has an effect by taking measurements before and afterward and comparing the results to a comparison or control group that did not get the intervention. Experiments always involve a comparison group. When there is no comparison group, but an intervention is assessed before and after, the design is called a "prepost design" (Campbell & Stanley, 1967).

EXAMPLE 4.6

USING EXPERIMENTAL DESIGN TO EVALUATE LANGUAGE ARTS PROGRAMS

A group of elementary teachers wanted to know which of four language arts programs was most effective for non-English-speaking immigrant children. They decided to run pilot studies to examine each of four possible series of materials. During the summer, they each underwent training in how to use one of the programs. Then, they recruited volunteer children from among the immigrant communities in the area and randomly assigned them to five different groups. Before they began the pilot program, they administered a test of English language ability to all of the volunteers. Four groups of children then received instruction in language arts, each using a different one of the four programs under discussion. The fifth group of children received no instruction at all. At the end of the summer, the teachers readministered the test of English language proficiency to all five groups and compared the results. They inferred that the program used by the group with the highest test scores was the most effective. They also assumed that the group receiving the lowest scores might be the group that received no language arts treatment at all.

EXAMPLE 4.7

USING EXPERIMENTAL DESIGN TO EVALUATE WOUND TREATMENT

A group of medical researchers was interested in determining which conditions best promoted the healing of superficial wounds: cleaned and exposed to air only; cleaned and bandaged; or cleaned, treated with antibiotic salve, and then bandaged. To determine which worked best in field conditions, patients with similar wound conditions were randomly assigned to groups, each of which was subjected to a different treatment condition. After a specified period of time, the healing rates were compared to see which worked best.

In the examples above, the intervention or treatment varied but the condition treated—lack of English proficiency and existence of wounds—remained the same. In a good experiment, the researchers try to make sure that the only difference between the subjects—or patients and students, in the examples above—is in the treatment they receive. In some experimental research, one group of subjects—the control group—will receive no treatment at all, or will receive whatever has been the standard or traditional treatment. Effectiveness of the treatment or intervention is measured by assessing differences across all groups, including the control group (which has received limited, standard, or no treatment), a specified time *after* the treatment or intervention has been implemented.[2]

Experimental researchers make every effort to be sure that both the administration of the intervention and the characteristics of participants in each of the groups are as similar as possible. In the first example above, results would not be valid if the children in one of the groups already had had some instruction in English or if one of the teachers were much more competent than the others. Similarly, the researchers' inferences about the effectivness of healing treatments could be questioned if the subjects in one treatment group were healthier or much younger than those in the other groups, because rapid healing could be attributed to health or age rather than to the experimental treatment.

Experimental researchers try to ensure comparability of groups by assigning subjects randomly to treatment groups. They ensure what is called "procedural validity"—or comparability of the treatment, innovation, or intervention—by developing highly structured protocols for the teachers, medical personnel (in the examples cited above), practitioners, or other individuals who supervise the treatments to use, and then training them in how to carry out the protocols and observe the results of the interventions. One limitation of experiments is that they usually must take place in a laboratory, clinical, or institutional setting; the kind of controlled and rigorous conditions required for true experimental designs—or even quasi-experimental designs (see Campbell & Stanley, 1963; Cook & Campbell, 1979; Reichardt & Cook, 1979)—rarely can be secured in the field.[3]

Controlled Field Studies or Quasi-Experiments

True control groups often cannot be created and differences among experimental subjects and in (or among) treatment administration(s) can lead to differences not legitimately produced by the intervention. Although random assignment of subjects can reduce this problem, obligations to clients in schools, social service agencies, public health clinics, and most other real-world settings often preclude random assignment. For example, federal laws in the United States preclude withholding educational services from children with special needs, so that if the pilot study described in Example 4.6 had been carried out in public schools during the regular school year, none of the children could have been excluded from language arts instruction. Researchers would have had to establish comparison or multiple treatment groups rather than a true control group. Similarly, in AIDS research, federal guidelines preclude the use of "no-treatment control groups." Thus, in a recent AIDS research project, "standard" and "enhanced" interventions were compared. The standard intervention was a culturally sensitive but nonethnically specific intervention for an ethnically mixed group, whereas the two enhanced interventions were specifically culturally targeted to African American injection drug users in one location and Puerto Rican injection drug users in the other (Weeks, Schensul, Williams, & Singer, 1995).

A modification of the true experiment—the controlled field study—finds great use in applied settings such as schools and clinics, where practitioners still want to know if their programs are effective or their hunches are valid but cannot maintain the kinds of control over subject characteristics and assignment found in a lab. Controlled field studies are implemented where random assignment is not possible, but considerable control over how procedures are implemented still can be obtained. They take place not in laboratories but in the natural habitat or customary environment of the participants.

EXAMPLE 4.8

A CONTROLLED FIELD STUDY OF AN ARTS EDUCATION PROGRAM

Centerfield Middle School wanted to set up an Arts Focus program that both integrated arts instruction with regular "hard" subjects and provided children with extended immersion in one of several arts disciplines. The school hired trained arts educators in Theater and Drama, Music, and Fine Arts and helped each of them to establish an integrated curriculum to be offered daily for 90 minutes throughout the year. Recognizing that some parents wanted their children to receive less intensive instruction in the arts, whereas others may prefer electives other than arts courses, the school plan was to establish three instructional streams: Arts Focus, Arts Electives, and Regular Electives. Students enrolled in Arts Focus took regular hard subjects plus a year-long, 90-minute arts class. Those in the Arts Electives stream enrolled in regular "hard" subjects plus semester-long, 55-minute elective classes in arts classes of their choice. Children in the Regular Electives stream simply enrolled in the traditional program, a mix of "hard" subjects and whatever semester-long electives they chose: arts classes or nonarts classes such as computer science, gardening, or chess club. The school wanted to compare the impact of participation in the various streams on both academic achievement and interest in school. They planned to collect regular achievement test data for all of the students before the school year starts, and to administer an attitudinal survey assessing how committed students were to their studies at the beginning of classes. They administered the survey and collected the test scores again at the end of each subsequent school year, matching the pre- and posttest scores for each of the children to assess changes over time.

Example 4.8 is a controlled field study; it takes place in the natural habitat of middle school children—a public school. It would be a *very* controlled study (a "true experimental study") if the children could be randomly assigned to each of the curricular streams, thus ensuring that differences among the groups would be minimized. However, because it is a public school, Centerfield must permit students—or their parents—to choose their particular elec-

tives stream. Notwithstanding, the streams themselves constitute quite different "treatments," and both the training received by teachers and the existence of a curriculum and instructional materials ensure a degree of **procedural validity.** Pre- and posttest measures also have been established, and the school's plan to aggregate matched individual scores on these measures ensures some degree of reliability in the results. Centerfield's teachers also can examine the characteristics of students in the different streams for differences in aptitudes, ability, gender, race, socioeconomic status, and other variables to permit more valid comparisons among the groups by controlling for these factors in analysis.

Definition: Procedural validity refers to the preciseness with which a study or an intervention is implemented according to its research design

Case control studies are another approach to quasi-experimental or controlled field study design. Case control studies are often done by epidemiologists interested in why disease or death occurs in one group but does not in another, presumably similar or even identical group. The term **case control** refers to the selection of cases fitting the study criteria in which the so-called problem is present, matched with similar controls in which the problem is absent. The objective is to determine what differences exist between these two groups that might explain the presence of the problem in the cases. The samples for case control studies are usually obtained through accrual—that is, as the instances of the problem occur in the selected population, they are included in the study sample, and a match, which does not show the presence of the problem at that time, is selected.

Definition: Case control refers to the selection of cases demonstrating the presence of a problem, matched with controls that have similar characteristics but in which the problem is absent

EXAMPLE 4.9

CASE CONTROL STUDY OF ACUTE RESPIRATORY INFECTION IN CHINA

Pneumonia is the most common killer of children between the ages of 0 and 5 in certain areas of China. The Chinese government, working with a government research center, the Capital Institute of Pediatrics in Beijing, set out to determine why. One strategy they chose was a case control study. To do this study, researcher Dai Yaohua chose a region of China in which reported deaths from pneumonia were especially high. Over the period of a year, she was able to accrue a hospital-based sample of approximately 400 households in which a child had died of pneumonia. As households with the death of a child in the target age group entered the sample, she was able to choose a matched sample in which a child of the same age with reported severe pneumonia survived. She was then able to determine, by systematically comparing households and disease history, what factors associated with the health history of the child, household demography and economics, beliefs about the disease, and beliefs about the health care system were most likely to contribute to mortality.

Table 4.2 summarizes the main features of experimental quasi-experimental groupings.

TABLE 4.2 Treatment, Comparison, and Control Groups

Treatment Group	Control Group	Comparison Group
— Participates in intervention or experiment — Subjects randomly selected for study and randomly assigned to group — Population characteristics and treatment conditions matched to control group	— Does not participate in intervention or experiment. May receive a traditional or customary treatment — Subjects randomly selected for study and randomly assigned to group — Population characteristics and treatment conditions matched to treatment group	— Participates in the same or a variant of the intervention or experiment, or in a different kind of intervention or experiment related to the research question — Subjects are not randomly assigned to treatment groups. Instead, they are assigned to treatment in naturally occurring groups (e.g., classrooms, work groups). These groups may be randomly selected and someimes are randomly assigned to treatment orcomparison conditions. — Population characteristics and/or or treatment conditions differ from treatment group, but differences are explicitly stated

Limitations on Controlled Field
Studies and Quasi-Experiments

Even in controlled field studies, where messiness caused by variability among the subjects themselves can be accounted for by matching participants and describing naturally occurring differences among the groups, procedures can go awry for a myriad of reasons, which leads to results not attributable to the treatment.

EXAMPLE 4.10

PROCEDURAL PROBLEMS IN A FIELD STUDY OF PLAYGROUND USE

The local Parks and Recreation Department was trying to reduce the incidence of aggressive behavior among children of different age groups who frequented the parks. A local sporting goods company offered to donate recreational equipment for use on the playgrounds if the Department would hire an aide to supervise its use. The Department staff agreed, and they planned to compare the number of police reports and parental complaints received from playgrounds with and without aides. Problems arose, however, and the program started late when a fiscal crisis prevented the aides from being hired until late July. At the end of the summer, there appeared to be no difference between the behavior observed among children at playgrounds with aides and those without. The sporting goods company deemed the program to be a failure and withdrew its support.

EXAMPLE 4.11

PROCEDURAL PROBLEMS IN A FIELD STUDY OF BILINGUAL EDUCATION

The number of Limited English Proficient students at Highlands Elementary School recently tripled. Sally Ames, a committed and creative teacher at the school, convinced her principal to let her establish a bilingual program that supported instruction in both Spanish and English for the students. After the first year, the principal transferred to another school, but Sally's enthusiasm had already convinced the remaining teachers in her school to learn Spanish and begin to implement a 3-year program of dual language instruction for all of the children in the school. The new principal somewhat reluctantly agreed to continue the experiment. However, while on a Caribbean scuba-diving vacation during the Christmas holidays, Sally drowned. Having lost both its inspirational leader and a supportive principal, the program faltered, and by the end of the second year, it had reverted to a more traditional program that used bilingual education for 2 or 3 years only, and only as a support to full-time instruction in English (Martinez, 1998).

Were either of these programs failures? Probably not. These kinds of crises, changes, and catastrophes are the reality of everyday life in the field. A limitation of experimental approaches or controlled field studies is that they assume that no factor other than the intervention could have produced the observed results. These approaches generally focus on measurement of outcomes. Without attention to careful documentation of the treatment process in addition to measurement of outcomes, they cannot provide any information about what factors—other than the intervention—could have influenced the results. Thus, the sporting goods company deemed the donation of its equipment to have been a failure, ignoring the fact that the program did not begin until the summer had nearly ended and before measurable differences among playgrounds could have accrued. Similarly, researchers trying to assess the effectiveness of the bilingual program after 3 years using only a pre-post test of proficiency in English and Spanish would declare the program ineffective—ignoring the loss of key personnel and the change in program design halfway through its implementation. For these reasons, ethnographic research directed to careful description of the program context and process is a necessary complement to quantitative research designs.

QUALITATIVE DESIGNS

Often, when things go well in experimental field research, ethnographic research adds important explanatory elements to the research design—as is the case in some of the situations described above, where researchers found that their designs did not match with conditions of life as they found it in the field, or when they could not force circumstances to conform to conditions and stipulations required for good experiments or controlled studies.

Cross Reference: See Examples 2.4, 4.1, 4.8, 4.10, 4.11

However, researchers can choose a different approach, changing the research question to better match the type of program or phenomenon that they plan to study. Rather than asking "Does this program work?" "Which is the best program?" or "Is this program effective?" they can ask questions such as the following:

- "What does program resilience mean, and how can we define and operationalize it?"
- "What is actually happening in the program?"
- "How does the program's history and what is happening in it contribute to the outcomes we observe?"
- "How can we explain the events and outcomes that *do* occur?"
- "*Why* is the program successful?"

For such questions, case studies—and ethnographies are culturally informed case studies—are appropriate because they allow us to assess and describe what really is happening

TABLE 4.3 Standard Qualitative Designs Used in the Social Sciences

	Minimal Conditions of Use
Case studies	— A population, process, problem, context, or phenomenon whose parameters and outcomes are unclear, unknown, or unexplored — An identified community, target population, or other unit of study
Ethnographies	— A population, process, problem, context, or phenomenon whose characteristics, parameters, or outcomes are unclear, unknown, or unexplored — Use of open-ended interviews and participant observation — A defined or operationalized group — A concern with using cultural concepts to guide the research and to help explain or interpret data
Narratives	— Individual(s) willing to tell stories or life, career, or personal histories — An interpretive framework based on the concepts and meanings used by the storyteller
Compressed designs: Rapid ethnographic assessments or focused ethnography	— A focused intervention problem — Brief studies of 3 days to 6 weeks — Use of a combination of elicitation techniques, focus groups, and key informant interviews to get information on a specific cultural domain needed for developing a culturally appropriate intervention
Action research	— Ethnographic research conducted in partnership with members of the community or setting in question with the specific purpose of bringing about structural or cultural change

after all, as well as what has been happening over time rather than at one point in time, or "pre and post." They also provide a way to document those events that impede or enhance success of participants' efforts (see Table 4.3).

Case Studies and Ethnographies

Case studies and ethnographies focus on a single unit for the investigation, whether it be an individual, as in clinical studies of mental or physical illness; a group, as in Example 4.1, which describes a study of dieters attending a particular weight loss clinic; or a single institution or program. Several examples above describe case studies of innovative educational programs. Example 5.5 involves a case study of a very complex, statewide program of competency testing for teachers. Studies of institutions might involve an entire school, corporation, or health care facility. Despite the complexity of the institutions and the number of individuals interviewed or surveyed, such studies still would be considered case studies because the "N"—or number of phenomena studied (communities or institutions)—is still just one.

Ethnographies are case studies because of their focus on a single entity, but they differ from case studies in general in that, as we have indicated in the first part of this book and in Table 4.3, they always include in their focus the *culture* of the group or entity under study. Other types of case studies—*not* ethnographies—include biographies; oral or clinical histories; and studies of innovations, group processes, organizational dynamics, or the characteristics of and interaction in any organization or group of people. Case studies usually are framed within a specific explanatory social or natural science discourse; a discipline such as psychology, history, or sociology, or an applied field such as social work, psychiatry, medicine, or education. That is why the TECAT program described in Example 5.5 is a case study and not an ethnography; it does emphasize process and description, but the description is not a cultural one. By contrast, the description of the Learning Circle Program presented in Examples 6.1 and 7.1 *is* derived from an ethnographic study because one of the key features of the investigation was the delineation of the culture of the participants and how it influenced the culture created in the program. Similarly, LeCompte's studies of Navajo school district (Examples 1.1 and 1.6) and Schensul's studies of children's activities and AIDS risk in Mauritius (Examples 1.4 and 6.2) also would be considered ethnographies because of their focus on the culture of the community in which the studies were situated.

Ethnographies and other forms of case studies always involve a consideration of people and events in their natural settings. They are, therefore, ideal for answering a question such as, "What's really happening in this program or with this individual?" The focus of such research, then, is on what makes the people in the study tick—how they behave, how they define their world, what is important to them, why they say and do what they do, and what structural or contextual features influence their thoughts, behaviors, and relationships.

Case study researchers and ethnographers typically live with or in the institutions or groups they are studying for extended periods of time because it takes considerable time to become acquainted with the participants; understand the dynamics of their interaction; understand how they relate to the physical and material environment; and elicit the meanings, goals, and objectives that are important to the participants. Ethnographies and other case studies all use participant observation and various forms of face-to-face, in-depth interviewing as principal forms of data collection. Consequently, they require that researchers develop considerable rapport with and trust among the people under study. Notwithstanding, they also employ many other different kinds of data collection as supplements to and corroboration for observations, such as the following:

- formal and informal interviews
- questionnaires
- standardized tests and measurements
- elicitation techniques
- archival records
- audio- and videotapes
- still photographs
- artifacts and maps

Cross Reference: These forms of data collection are discussed in Books 2, 3, and 4

Typically, ethnographers and other case study researchers observe and talk to members of a group to find out what the members are doing and why. They try not to take for granted anything they see or hear, always cross-checking their own perceptions and conclusions with information from research participants. Then, they assemble all of the information that they have collected into descriptions of relationship and recurring patterns of behavior and belief so that a full portrait of the group can be constructed.

Narratives

Definition: Narrative inquiry is the study of people's stories that involves creating, collecting, and analyzing written texts

In recent years, some researchers have come to study single individuals in a kind of research called **narrative inquiry**. Anthropology has a long history of using the accounts of single individuals, commonly called "key informants" (or cultural experts), to develop a picture of the beliefs and practices of a community. Key informants typically are chosen because they are quite knowledgeable about their own culture (and also are willing and able to communicate with anthropologists). Anthropologists also use life histories to understand the role and experience of individuals who are often unique in their time and setting. It is also common for anthropologists to collect narratives, or accounts of specific experiences (e.g., narratives of entry into drug use, or narratives describing the most recent experiences in treating a health problem or managing encounters with teachers in a child's school). In general, narratives of all sorts constitute text data that provide rich descriptions of particular events, situations, or personal histories.

Although the stories told by key informants may, in some respects, resemble those told by participants in a narrative study, the purposes for which they are told differ dramatically. The anthropologist's focus remains on the culture of the group; the stories told by key informants are only nominally the stories of that particular individual. Rather, they are used by the anthropologist to *typify* the behaviors and beliefs of the group. The narratives in narrative studies, by contrast, have no necessary similar cultural referent; they are taken to represent the experience of the individual alone.

Strictly speaking, narratives involve human experience, although they can be constructed from a variety of sources. Sometimes, these texts originate in books as articles; they can be created from plays, court transcripts, films, and videotapes, or even from the stage directions used to direct such productions. However, most often they are generated by individuals in the course of talking about or recording their life experiences. They usually start out in the form of entries in diaries or journals, or as interview transcripts or oral histories elicited by researchers. A relatively new form of research design, narratives obtained from different people and sources can be used to assemble a composite picture of a group's experiences.

Narratives focus on knowledge, beliefs, and practices; they are used to study how people practice their professions, how they learn to carry out tasks, and how they come to know about their world. They are also used to highlight the experiences of people who have been oppressed or marginalized where they live. In the latter cases, narratives often are defined as "giving voice" to people whose experiences are not well known in the mainstream of their society. Finally, narratives can be used to present multiple perspectives in a given setting (Clifford & Marcus, 1986).

There are many kinds of narratives. Commonly, they consist of more or less chronological accounts of a person's life, career, or set of experiences. They can, however, be obtained from transcripts of courtroom or other formal proceedings; stories of people's intention to do something or explanations of why they acted as they did; series of episodes, fantasies, or philosophical musings. They may or may not reflect the structure of what has been called "grand narrative," with plot, setting, characters, conflict, conflict resolution, and a moral or summing up (Heath, 1996).

Particularly when talking with individuals whose culture is not informed by Western European and North American grand narratives, or with youth whose peer groups actively reject such narrative structure, ethnographers need to take care not to impose such structures on the discourse of participants—if, in fact, what is desired is the discourse style of the participant (see LeCompte, 1997, for a discussion of the pitfalls involved in such imposition).

Some research theorists argue that narrative by itself does not constitute a research design. Rather, they hold that narrative is a data collection technique that can be used fruitfully in a variety of research designs, including oral historiography, ethnography, and case studies. Notwithstanding, we include narrative here as a design primarily because it has become so widely used, especially in the fields of education and of ethnic and gender studies, to call attention to details of practice as well as to the experiences of marginalized individuals.

Compressed Ethnographic Research Designs

There are many occasions when resources of time, money, and staff do not permit conduct of a full-fledged ethnography, even though it is clear that an ethnography would be the most appropriate design. In these cases, some methodologists have designed modifications of traditional ethnography that accommodate to shortened time lines and/or multiple sites (e.g., Pelto & Gove, 1992; Scrimshaw & Gleason, 1992; Scrimshaw & Hurtado, 1985).

Compression is possible under certain circumstances: First, the ethnographers must already be familiar with the field setting and/or the cultural context, and, ideally, speak the language. Indeed, that particular setting may be in their own home community. Second, the work must be focused on one aspect of the culture. It should not attempt to cover a wide spectrum of beliefs and behaviors in different cultural domains. For example, focused ethnographic studies can be conducted on symptoms of infant diarrhea for purposes of improving diagnosis and treatment (but not on childhood diseases in general), or on environmental barriers to millet production (but not on barriers to agricultural production in general). Third, ethnographers should work with cultural experts from the setting even if they share national origin with research participants. Ethnographers may not be familiar with the local setting; working with local experts or partners speeds the work and ensures validity. These partners can assist in establishing the context for the data collection, participate in designing the research, and interpret the results. This can avoid mistakes resulting from the researchers' lack of familiarity with the setting.

In compressed research designs, data collection techniques must be suitable to convenient use in a brief period of time. Favored for this purpose are cognitive elicitation techniques, such as listing and pilesorts, group interviews with representative samples of individuals, in-depth interviews with cultural experts or key informants, and brief surveys administered to small representative samples. Triangulation of these multiple data sources is necessary to produce a comprehensive and consistent picture of a specific cultural domain.

Cross References:
See Book 3, Chapter 1 on elicitation techniques

See Book 3, Chapter 2 on focused group interviews

See Book 2 on surveys

━●━●━ **EXAMPLE 4.12**

TRIANGULATION IN A MULTISITE RAPID ASSESSMENT OF NUTRITION AND PRIMARY CARE

Anthropologist Susan Scrimshaw reported on a United Nations University-funded, 16-site investigation in nutrition and primary care conducted from a household perspective. Group interviews (conversations on an informal basis with informants or small groups) and focus groups (small, homogeneous groups gathered for group discussions of appropriate research topics) were part of the repertoire of data collection techniques used in this rapid assessment project.

Triangulation involved repeated questions, discussion, and actual observation, look-ing for the same information or information on the same topic. In terms of sampling, it was not efficient to seek random samples. The study focused on poor and rural households with children under 5 years of age. Random sampling was possible only in nine countries. Purposive or opportunistic sampling was more feasible, and "concerns for representativeness could be honored by a strong awareness of what was typical or deviant for the culture." Also, "families could be added to the sample if more seemed necessary because of a wide variability in responses." Scrimshaw notes that "the RAP is best done by researchers either from or familiar with the cultural setting who are starting with an already existing good basis of information." But, she cautions, even where researchers are local (i.e., nationals), communities may be wary of outsiders" (Scrimshaw, 1992, p. 31).

⬤━⬤━⬤

Action Research

Some researchers define *action research* broadly as any research conducted with a clear institutional or community structural change in mind. Others reserve the term for research designed to address structural inequalities, such as limited or poor quality mental health services for poor rural residents, gaps in computer and library resources in urban schools, or preferential hiring in private hospitals in urban areas of Sri Lanka. Regardless, action research is site-specific and involves researchers and participants who jointly par-ticipate in four specific steps: (a) the identification of a problem, (b) the joint conduct of research to gain a better understanding of the problem, (c) joint analysis of research results, and (d) taking action to remedy the problem. Re-searchers and participants engage in all of these steps, in-cluding joint action, as partners (Schensul & Schensul, 1978; Stringer, 1996). The following example illustrates the interaction of these steps.

EXAMPLE 4.13

USING RAPID ASSESSMENT AND ACTION RESEARCH TO
ESTABLISH A WOMEN'S HEALTH INITIATIVE IN INDIA

Kanani describes a project in India that combined the use of rapid assessment procedures with action research. A nongovernmental organization interested in folk perceptions of women's morbidity as the backdrop for establishing a women's health initiative began a project in two urban, low-income slum areas differing by religion; one was Muslim and one was Hindu. An important outcome of the project was expected to be the establishment of a health center for women in each slum; this was a strongly felt local need: "Open a health center for us and you will know all about our health problems."

The sample included married women between the ages of 20 and 50 with at least one child who were likely to have heard about women's illnesses arising from marriage and motherhood. Center staff used a combination of focus groups, free listing and pilesorting, ethnographic interviews, narratives, and key informant interviews for the study. There were 19 group interviews with about 15 women in each group. The focus group discussions were to build rapport with women and to outline the general framework of women's morbidity—types, etiology, and treatment.

At first, researchers carried out informal interviews with naturally forming groups (or networks) in neighborhoods. Later groups were systematically formed by including an equal number of older (age 40 and up) and younger (ages 20-30) women in neighborhood-based groups of approximately 15 to 18 women. The group discussions helped to build rapport with women and provided a framework for their health problems, including reproductive health. Participants encouraged their neighbors to describe their problems freely, thus providing considerable data on women's morbidity, local terms used, and perceived etiologies and treatment patterns. Participants in focus groups located women leaders to help out with research and subsequent planning for health services, and to decide priorities for subsequent research (Kanani, 1992).

Ethnography is very useful in the first stages of an action research project to help in defining the problem, the cultural setting, and the action research partners. The most important consideration in conducting responsible action research is that the results are likely to be subjected to scrutiny by multiple audiences and critics: the research partners, research participants, public and private institutions, the media, and the scientific community. Because so much rests on valid and reliable results, great pains must be taken to ensure the rigor of the research and the appropriateness of the research design to all audiences. If one of the main audiences for the research will believe only the results of a survey, focus group research will not result in a successful outcome. For action research to end in the desired change, ethnographers must do an ethnography of both the problem and its social and political context for change.

The Interaction of Qualitative and Quantitative Designs

We said earlier in this chapter that qualitative and quantitative research designs are not mutually exclusive. Some researchers prefer to maintain separation of designs—they are purists, doing either qualitative or quantitative work. We believe, though, that features of qualitative and quantitative designs can complement and strengthen each other. Tables 4.4 and 4.5, respectively, summarize some of the main ways that qualitative and quantitative design features can be integrated as readers plan their research designs.

Now that we have discussed the design options available to ethnographers as they begin their work, we turn in the next chapter to a discussion of the decision-making process that researchers use to choose ethnographic designs and the strategies employed to design them.

TABLE 4.4 The Interaction of Qualitative Research Methods With Quantitative Research Designs

Quantitative Design Type	Role of Ethnography in Quantitative Research Designs
Cross-sectional research: Population and sample surveys	*Preparation for survey* — Identification of the problem and context — Identification of the range of responses — Identification of target population, characteristics, locations, and possible barriers to survey research *Complementary data* — Identification and exploration of social subgroups, explaining patterned variation in survey results
Experiments	*Preparation* — Identification of elements of the experiment — Identification of constraints in field — Pilot testing for acceptability and feasibility — Developing and validating measures of change *Process* — Finding differences in implementation — Documenting content of intervention for comparison with outcome measures
Controlled field studies/ quasi-experiments	*Preparation* — Identification of elements of the treatment — Identification of potential differences among treatment and control groups — Identification of constraints to experimentation in the field — Pilot testing for acceptability and feasibility — Developing and validating measures of change *Process* — Finding differences in implementation — Documenting content of intervention for comparison with outcome measures

TABLE 4.5 The Interaction of Quantitative Methods With Qualitative Research Designs

Qualitative Research Designs	Role of Quantitative Research in Relation to Ethnography
Case studies/ethnographies	— Survey to confirm and validate ethnographically defined patterns — "Case-control" matched sample to identify factors associated with presence/absence of element (e.g., disease, school performance, etc.)
Ethnographies	— Survey to confirm and validate ethnographically defined patterns — "Case-control" matched sample to identify factors associated with presence/absence of element (e.g., disease, school performance, etc.) — Time series design (repeated observations of the same units over time) to define change more accurately
Narratives	— Survey to demonstrate presence of patterns revealed by narratives, using language and concepts of respondents
Compressed or rapid ethnographic assessments or focused ethnography	— Brief cross-sectional surveys with small samples — Brief pre-post surveys and panel designs for assessing intervention
Action research	— Action research makes use of both qualitative and quantitative design features to accomplish the purpose designated by the problem and the partnership

NOTES

1. *Validity* has several meanings. At its broadest, validity refers to the "goodness," authenticity, credibility, and quality of the research (Lincoln & Guba, 1985). In experimental research, *internal* validity refers to the degree to which what happens in an experiment can be attributed to the experimental intervention that is the focus of the study (Campbell & Stanley, 1963; LeCompte & Preissle, 1993; Porter, 1978). In sample surveys and in experiments for which populations are chosen randomly, validity also refers to how accurately the results obtained describe the larger population from which the study sample was drawn (Campbell & Stanley, 1963; Jaeger, 1978; LeCompte & Preissle, 1993; Porter, 1978).

2. In many cases, researchers cannot establish a real control group because it would be unethical not to treat people who are, for example, injured or in need of a program. For this reason, many medical and educational programs use multiple comparison groups rather than the traditional control group. Example 4.7, as a case in point, includes multiple comparison groups because no patient went untreated. The researchers in Example 4.6, however, *could* have a real control group because their experiment was an optional summer

program. The control group was not deprived of regular classroom instruction.

3. Notwithstanding, randomized assignment to treatment and control groups, and educational counseling or prevention interventions that are standardized in curriculum or other instructional manuals, now often can be found in field or community settings as well as in laboratory-like settings. Situations calling for standardized intervention manuals include treatment and prevention of HIV/AIDS and sexually transmitted diseases, pregnancy prevention, and interventions with people with mental health and drug abuse diagnoses.

5 ━━●━━●━━

CHOOSING AND DESIGNING AN ETHNOGRAPHIC RESEARCH PROJECT

We already have discussed the characteristics of ethnography and its paradigms and purposes in Chapters 1 through 3, and in Chapter 4, we discussed design options that ethnographers can use. To summarize what we have said so far, if the purpose of the research project is to

- Determine the characteristics of a population
- Define a social problem
- Figure out which problems need solving
- Describe how individuals in a group interpret their worlds
- Present what people do and why
- Provide information that will assist in planning a project
- Document a process
- Provide ongoing feedback to practitioners
- Monitor implementation, or find out what is going on
- Provide information that will help to interpret or explain outcomes

then ethnography is an appropriate choice.

As we have described earlier, ethnographic investigators tend to examine very complex phenomena. Consequently, ethnographic research designs tend to be rather complex, if only because they tend to involve a number of quite different kinds of people and a variety of information sources, and to take place over time. All of these factors create opportunities for felicitous surprises—or miserable mishaps. Of course, individual projects will vary in complexity depending on what the investigator is trying to find out. Therefore, the first thing a researcher should do once the basic question or idea to be investigated is known is to create a **research design** for the project.

Definition:
A research design is an overall plan for conducting a research project covering all steps—from raising the research questions through data analysis

Key point

Even though the ethnographic process has built into it a good deal of flexibility and intuitive activity, it is not a haphazard, serendipitous, or playful activity. In fact, its very spontaneity mandates a good solid substructure or framework. A research design provides this framework or substructure. *All good ethnographers try to create an overall design in which anticipated details and activities are spelled out as far as current information permits.* This includes activities that occur throughout the project, as well as those that are usually thought of as taking place at the end, such as how data will be analyzed and results disseminated, and how the research team will disengage from participants and say good-bye. Of course, this does not mean that research designs are etched in stone, or that the conduct of ethnographic research follows a logical linear sequence—quite the contrary. Designs—and researchers—need to remain sufficiently flexible to allow for contingencies.

An ethnographic research design needs to begin with a set of decisions about what the goals of the project are to be. It then can accommodate new opportunities for exploration, changes of direction, surprises, and emergencies while also keeping researchers congruent with the original goals of the project. If, as often happens in ethnographic research, new goals are added or old goals are reformulated during the course of the project, the design should change to accommodate these goal changes as the project evolves. Just as the date of a traveler's return or the airline he or she uses for a trip might change from that initially set out by a travel agency, research activities also change in response to unforeseen conditions. Unless the researcher—or vacationer—has at least thought through an initial itinerary or set of activities and considered possible alternatives, luck alone will determine whether either investigators or travelers complete their projects as planned and arrive unscathed.

Unlike hapless vacationers, whose changes in plans simply leave them happy to be home, researchers must make sure that the reasons for change as well as the changes themselves can be accounted for and articulated fully each time circumstances call for modifications in their research design. If they cannot, the project will grow increasingly haphazard, and the results will be equally haphazard in the end. In the worst-case scenario, the study will produce no worthwhile results at all.

DECIDING WHAT TO INVESTIGATE

Research designs follow the same questions that guide the work of most social science researchers or good investigative reporters—"What?" "Where?" "Who?" "When?" "How?" and "Why?" We now describe how ethnographers begin to answer these questions.

Deciding "What" to Investigate: Where Do Research Topics or Questions Come From?

Research designs begin with questions that researchers and their partners want to answer about a particular problem, population, process, or project; or with topics they want to explore. Community groups, teachers, or health care providers who find themselves in need of information can also identify research questions or topic areas.

Key point

EXAMPLE 5.1

SELECTION BY RESEARCH SITE: AN ARTS
EDUCATION PROGRAM SOLICITS AN EVALUATION

A middle school in a midwestern community decided to set up an arts program that would provide all of its students with an intensive exposure to theater, music, and the literary and visual arts. The lead teacher contacted a researcher at the nearby state university to assist in doing a study of the program, knowing that evaluative information would help the school in seeking funding for the coming year, and that documentary evidence of successes and failures would assist the teachers in improving the program over time.

In this case, teachers in the field situation identified the general topic for the study, but the research questions needed to be specified and clarified by teachers and researchers working together.

Key point   *Research questions also may come from the brainstorming of collaborative groups, or the specific interests and commitments of anyone involved in formulating the question.* For example, one group of mothers in a training program for women in Hartford, Connecticut, wanted to

Cross Reference:
See Book 7, Chapter 2

know whether a program for mothers and daughters would make a difference in helping young girls to avoid sex- and drug-related risks. This led to the creation of a 5-year program to actually test this question (cf. Schensul, Berg, & Romero, 1997).

Many researchers who come from minority, oppressed, or stigmatized groups choose to study the experiences of their own groups. For example, Andrea O'Conor (1993/1994), an educational researcher who is also a lesbian, has studied the development of gender identity in gay and lesbian youth; Concha Delgado-Gaitan (1988) and many other Latino/a researchers who remember their own negative experiences in school have documented how treatment in schools leads Mexican-American and Latino/a children to academic failure. Evelyn Phillips, an African American

urban anthropologist, studies the construction, decon-
struction, and forced migration of African American and
other urban communities (Phillips, 1996).

EXAMPLE 5.2

SELECTION BY RESEARCH SITE: A COMMUNITY COALITION INITIATES A STUDY

When informed by Centers for Disease Control (CDC) colleagues in 1986 that the
pattern of HIV/AIDS transmission was shifting from infection via sexual contact to
infection via drug use, a coalition of community organizations in Hartford, Connecticut, representing several different ethnic/racial groups, decided to mount a
series of studies to find out how accurate the CDC's report was. The purpose of the
research was to provide information that might prevent the spread of AIDS among
intravenous drug users in Hartford's communities (Schensul, 1999; Schensul et al.,
1999; Singer, 1999).

For many researchers, questions arise out of the tasks in   **Key point**
which they engage at their own workplace. Others develop
from requests for research by specific agencies or organizations. Private philanthropists and foundations, for example, often sponsor research congruent with the interests of
their supporters.

EXAMPLE 5.3

SELECTION BY INTERESTED PARTY: INITIATION OF CANCER RESEARCH BY A CANCER SURVIVOR

A successful Utah-based businessman donated several million dollars to the University of Utah to establish a cancer research institute. The businessman and many
members of his entire extended family had suffered from unusually high rates of
cancer. Dissatisfied with the success rates of cancer treatments, he charged the newly
established institute with finding cures for the disease.

In a similar, Connecticut-based example, consistent with the
will of its founder, the Ethel P. Donaghue Medical Foundation
offered opportunities for research in cardiovascular problems
and diabetes.

Key point   *Researchers also may find that funding initiatives gener-ate new questions.* Current medical research is heavily in-fluenced by the kinds of funding available; HIV/AIDS, can-cer, and heart disease, for example, are the most heavily funded—and therefore studied—diseases in the United States, notwithstanding that many other diseases affect just as many people. By contrast, disease prevention, which receives little money from governmental or private sources, has received correspondingly little attention from re-searchers. Similarly, funders of educational research shape research directions.

It is important to note, however, that funders can and do shift their attention to new areas of concern when the public campaigns for support in these areas. For example, public advocacy in the United States created widespread support for drug prevention research, which resulted in the found-ing of the federal Center for Substance Abuse Prevention in 1987. In response, a scholarly infrastructure that was fo-cused on prevention research arose practically overnight. This infrastructure has included several national and inter-national interdisciplinary research organizations, federally funded prevention research centers, and a commitment from national foundations that are involved in health issues to fund prevention programs.

 Key point   *Scholarly or personal commitments also generate re-search questions.* It is important to recognize that despite myths about the objective nature of scientific investigation, research projects are always, to some degree, affected by the personal training, preferences, political views, experiences, and even the neuroses of the investigators carrying them out. People choose to do the kinds of research and to explore particular research questions that are compatible with what they value; with their own views about the nature of reality; with what constitutes truth; and with how knowledge is most appropriately sought, verified, and put to use. They also interpret data in accordance with the ideas and concepts that they find meaningful in professional training, either as scholars or researchers or as practitioners in their particular field. Thus, for example, without additional social science training, people trained in medicine are less likely to focus on the psychosocial and emotional correlates of disease. Psychologists, by contrast, may tend to ignore the possible physiological origins of neurosis and psychosis. Educators trained to look at whether or not an instructional technique produced the desired effect will be more inclined to focus on the *process* of what happened when they have had training in anthropology.

Once a researcher has identified an initial interest or problem area, he or she then begins the process of transforming a very broad and often vague problem area into a series of quite concrete elements of research design:

- *What:* The specific issues and research questions related to the problem area
- *Why:* The reasons or rationale for focusing on this area
- *Where:* The place or site where the study can be conducted
- *With Whom:* The categories of people with whom the problem could best be studied
- *When:* The time span needed to conduct the study
- *How:* The way in which the information can be located and collected
- *Who:* Which people can provide access to the site, people, or sources for information needed to answer the question

The Importance of Collaboration With People in the Field

It is at this point that collaboration with people in the field becomes crucial. If it has not already been initiated during the course of identifying the initial problem area, then the researcher needs to establish these relationships immediately. Collaboration with people in the field is crucial during initial phases of the design process, especially if the researcher is an outsider hired to conduct the study or is doing it as an independently funded investigator. External researchers may be relatively familiar with the particular type of project and its internal workings, but they will not know who the participants, service providers, or clients are; exactly how records are kept; who has access to what kinds of information; and who is willing to talk with whom at the specific site. Even researchers who are working collaboratively as insiders or semi-insiders will need to ask a lot of questions of others to ensure that the research problems explored are ones relevant to the people in the project, that the data collection strategies delineated in the research design are workable, and that the analysis and dissemination plans are both reasonable and effective.

Cross Reference:
See Chapter 6, Table 6.2 for an example of how these questions are laid out in a "data collection matrix"

ELABORATING RESEARCH QUESTIONS

Following is a case study of how an initial problem area was elaborated into a series of questions that established the basis for what to study (i.e., formed the framework for a research design).

➤━━●━━●━━━

Case Study

ELABORATION OF AN INITIAL PROBLEM AREA INTO RESEARCH QUESTIONS ABOUT URBAN AMERICAN INDIAN CHILDREN: THE LEARNING CIRCLE PROGRAM

Margaret LeCompte was approached by the Educational Director of the Phoenix Indian Center to help develop an evaluation plan for a program for which the director was seeking governmental funding: The Learning Circle, an after-school cultural and educational enrichment program for urban American Indian elementary school children. LeCompte agreed to help with the project because of her interest in the education of ethnic minority children in general, and American Indians in particular. The initial problem was to develop a way to evaluate a project that had not yet begun. The director sent LeCompte the completed program plan and asked her to address two areas: how to (a) describe what had happened during the project's 3 years, and (b) determine what impact, if any, the program had had on the children during that time. These general areas had to be broken down into descriptive questions about program operations and assessment questions about the program's impact.

The first set of descriptive questions involved finding out who the participants in the programs were.

- Who was the Project Director? Why was she selected? What was her background, training, and philosophy?
- Who were the teachers who were involved, and what were their background, training, and philosophy?
- How many students were enrolled? How were they selected, and what were their characteristics and backgrounds?
- How many parents participated? What were their backgrounds and reasons for enrolling their children?

The second set of descriptive questions involved what was going on in the substantive part of the program: planning meetings, classroom instruction, home visits, parent activities, and field trips.

- Where and in how many schools was the program located?
- What kinds of activities occurred in the classrooms? On home visits? At parent meetings? On field trips? How many children and parents participated in these activities?
- What did the teachers do to organize and plan their activities?
- What was their curriculum?
- What problems occurred during the course of the program's implementation?

Program impact (the second area of concern) also had to be assessed. The researchers and staff decided to define impact in two ways: First, how did people feel about the program? Second, did participation in the program produce any noticeable changes in the children it served? The first question—how people felt about the program—was further broken down in terms of "stakeholders" or participants, as follows:

- How do the *children* feel about The Learning Circle?
- How do the *parents* feel about their children's and their own participation in the program?
- How do the *teachers and aides* feel about the program?
- What attitudes do the *principals and administrative staff* of the district have about the program?

The second assessment question regarding behavioral changes in children in the program was defined in terms of academic achievement and school attendance; it was broken down as follows:

- Have Learning Circle students shown greater gains on the standardized achievement tests administered in the district than comparable groups of other children who were not enrolled in The Learning Circle?
- Do Learning Circle students exhibit higher levels of attendance than students who are not enrolled in the program?

In the course of collecting these data, it became apparent that all participants in the program were profoundly affected by the cultural emphasis of the program in ways that were not tapped by the questions above. This led to further questions:

- What special emphases and practices does Learning Circle have that other enrichment programs do not have?
- How do American Indian staff from multiple tribal groups develop a cultural curriculum that could serve children from many different tribes?
- How do the Learning Circle staff translate values common to American Indian culture into instructional activities?
- How do the teachers resolve their own interethnic conflicts during planning sessions?
- What differences do teachers and parents notice in the demeanor of Learning Circle children before and after they have enrolled in the program?

The answers to these questions led the program staff and the researchers to still others:

- How can a culturally informed program be strengthened by integrating it with innovative new ways of thinking about how children learn?
- Can a program like The Learning Circle be used with multi-ethnic populations other than American Indians?

━●━●━

This example shows how research questions can evolve from ones that seem relatively straightforward and descriptive into others that become increasingly complex and more deeply informed by theory. The following is a case study from another project that illustrates a similar process.

━●━●━

**EVOLUTION OF A RESEARCH PROBLEM FROM
CONCRETE TO THEORETICALLY INFORMED QUESTIONS:
MANAGING DIABETES AMONG PUERTO RICAN IMMIGRANTS**

Case Study

Researcher Henrietta Bernal joined forces with the Institute for Community Research to conduct studies of diabetes management among older Puerto Rican adults in the Hartford area. While carrying out these studies, researchers noted that most of the patients were women between the ages of 60 and 85. Could diabetes be related to migration, length of time in the city, or changing dietary patterns? During the course of research, it became clear that exercise was not part of the daily program of these women. Researchers began to ask a series of questions:

- Why did women not engage in what researchers called "exercise" even when they had the opportunity to do so; and what did they do in the way of energy expenditure instead?
- Could dietary continuities be found from childhood to adulthood, linked to early onset of adult type II diabetes?
- Was migration related to early onset of type II diabetes?

- Did women believe that diabetes could be managed more effectively and early onset prevented?
- What were women communicating to their children regarding the likelihood of contracting diabetes and whether or not it could be prevented?
- Did women link diabetes with other chronic diseases of adulthood such as arthritis and cardiovascular problems?

The research team began to question whether behavioral and structural antecedents to diabetes could be found among younger women in the same community. Prior research on infant and toddler feeding patterns pointed to the early and consistent intake of foods with high sugar, starch, salt, and fat content. Less understood and equally important in diabetes prevention and management is exercise. But researchers knew nothing about activity levels in either older adults or children. They began to ask new questions.

- In what activities did children engage?
- Were there differences among children within the same age group with respect to activities?
- Were different energy levels associated with different types of activities?
- To what extent did parent, peer, school, or environmental factors influence energy expenditures in younger children?
- Could these factors somehow be related to socialization practices and parental modeling in the household and the community?

The answers to these questions were available for working-class white children, who were the target population for the Framingham Children's Heart Health Study but they were not available for urban Puerto Rican or African American children. Nor were instruments available that could be considered culturally or contextually appropriate for use with these groups.

Researchers at the Institute mounted a pilot study designed to develop and test instruments, determine the range of variation in energy outputs among Puerto Rican children between the ages of 7 and 10, test an activities recall questionnaire against a mechanical measure of energy outputs to determine how accurately children could report in what activities they engaged; and assess peer, environmental, and parental socialization factors as possible influences on choice and frequency of daily activities and energy expended. The gender-specific results of this study produced more questions:

- What really influenced young girls to choose indoor activities with limited energy outputs?
- To what extent do gender differences in socialization influence girls' and boys' behaviors, and at what age do these differences become significant?
- In what ways does gender intersect with migration, acculturation, and environmental factors (structural flaws in building construction that inhibit exercise-related activities, perception of gang or street violence, fear of sexual harassment) to limit options for girls and young women?
- What is the relationship of these factors to mental health and prevention of chronic diseases in adult women?

➤•➤•➤

Having decided *what* needs to be known, the researcher can begin to work out specifics of how the research questions can be answered.

SELECTING POPULATIONS
AND UNITS OF ANALYSIS

After deciding more specifically in what ways to focus the study, the next step involves figuring out with whom and where the study can be done. Often, the phenomenon or population to be studied cannot be defined without at the same time identifying an accessible site where it can be found. Thus, these two questions involve interrelated and overlapping decisions. Recognizing the inseparability of

these issues, we nevertheless begin our discussion somewhat artificially by discussing how researchers choose the
population for a study.

What Is a Population?

Definition:
Population
refers to the group in
which the researcher
is interested; the unit
of analysis is the
individual element
or component
aggregated to
constitute the study
population

The term **population** refers to the entire group in which
a researcher is interested. Populations are usually made up
of human beings, but they can also constitute communities,
organizations, programs, animals, places, things, time periods, documents, words, phrases, sentences or paragraphs in
interview texts and transcripts, specific activities or bits of
behavior, and other such units.

Ethnographers usually study populations of people. The
study of so-called intact or isolated groups, typically carried
out by anthropologists in the first half of the 20th century,
made the task of defining a population much easier: the
population was synonymous with the cultural group. However, few such groups exist any more—if, indeed, they ever
did[1]—and even where groups do exist in relative isolation
from Western European influences, problems of access,
ethics, cultural self-determinism, and other political concerns make it difficult for ethnographers to study them.
Most often, ethnographers study groups of people embedded within larger communities, which are defined by the
characteristics or attributes that the individuals in the
group possess.

Establishing Logistical, Definitional, and
Conceptual Criteria for Selecting a Population

Researchers have many reasons for selecting the groups
they study. The first step in the selection of the study
population involves determining *why* the group should be
selected in the first place. The second step involves estab-

lishing a set of inclusion criteria or a list of characteristics that the members of the population need to have in order to be eligible for the study. Then, researchers must go looking for people or things that possess those characteristics. Selection criteria address logistical, definitional, and conceptual considerations.

Logistical criteria stem from the resources available for the study. However wonderful from a conceptual perspective it might be to include certain individuals, a cost-benefit analysis of the time, money, and distance needed to include them can make it clear that they should be excluded. A longitudinal study of physical growth and nutritional status in Puerto Rican children may require excluding those who move to Puerto Rico during the study period because of the cost of tracking them.

Definitional criteria determine how the group will be bounded and who is included in it. Considerations of inclusivity involve how many of the group members can be studied by the researcher given the needs of the study and available time and financial resources. For example, researchers studying drug use in adolescents may determine membership in the study group by age, ethnicity, location, or other criteria. Financial limitations of the study and ability to locate the study sample will influence decisions about sample size.

Conceptual criteria address the issue of saturation; saturation involves whether or not the proposed study group contains or exemplifies a sufficient number of members with the characteristics of interest to the researcher. A study of functional disability among older African American adults in a small city is important, but finding enough participants in a small population of adults over 50 may make the study impossible to pursue.

Researchers need to consider all three criteria. Figure 5.1 summarizes the logistical criteria, definitional and saturation criteria, and conceptual criteria that researchers need to consider in selecting a population.

LOGISTICAL CONSIDERATIONS

Has the group asked me to study it?
OR
Do I have to find a group to study?

IF I HAVE TO FIND A GROUP TO STUDY,

— Can I find a group with the attributes in which I am interested?
— Can I get permission to study the group?
— If I get permission to study the group, will its individual members talk to me?
OR
— Are people who have the characteristics or attributes in which I am interested not members of a known group?

ONCE I HAVE A GROUP AND PERMISSION TO STUDY IT,

— Do I have the resources to do a study with this group?
— Can I study all members of the group? Do I need to?
 I will need to if:
    the group is very heterogenous and I might miss an important member if I don't; or
    if its characteristics are unknown; or
    if the group is very small.

OR WILL I HAVE TO MAKE DESIGN DECISIONS BASED ON THE FOLLOWING:

— How far away or difficult to access is the group?
— How big is the group? Too big to study in its entirety?
— How difficult is it to identify the members?
— Do I have sufficient time and trained personnel to implement the study?

DEFINITIONAL CONSIDERATIONS

IF THE PEOPLE OF INTEREST ARE NOT MEMBERS OF A KNOWN GROUP,

— How can I bound or operationally define them for study?
AND
— Can I define a place, site, or organization where I might find them?
OR
— Can I identify a group or individual who might help me identify them?
— Once I have identified them, will they talk with me?

CONCEPTUAL CONSIDERATIONS

— Do I want to study representative members of the group? If so, are the characteristics of the population known well enough to identify such members?
OR
— Do I intend to compare the people or group that I want to study with other people or groups? If so, do I want to study typical, extreme, unique, ideal, negative, bellwether, or exemplary cases (see LeCompte & Preissle, 1993)?
— Or do I want to study a sample of the larger group?
— If I study a sample, how shall I construct it?

Figure 5.1. Selection criteria.

*Theoretical Sampling, or Selecting
for Conceptual Considerations*

The following strategies are included in the criterion-based selection of sample units:

■ Extreme or dichotomous case selection

■ Typical case selection

■ Unique case selection

■ Reputational case selection

■ Bellwether or ideal case selection

■ Comparable case selection

Ethnographic researchers use a number of systematic, nonrandomized approaches to select the individuals (or other units) they want to study. The first strategy is called **criterion-based selection** (LeCompte & Preissle, 1993), in which researchers choose individuals to study because they possess characteristics that match those of interest to the researchers. The first set of criterion-based selection procedures (see below: extreme, typical, and unique case selection) is used to determine patterns of difference between members of a population. Other types of criterion-based selection (reputational, bellwether or ideal case, comparable case) are then used if they are needed to further illuminate the research questions. Below, we define the principal types of criterion-based selection most commonly used in social science research.

Definition: Criterion-based selection involves choosing study participants because they possess characteristics related to the study's central questions

1. **Extreme or dichotomous case selection.** The researcher first defines a characteristic or interest using a scale by which individuals can be arrayed in accordance with how much of that characteristic they possess. The result is a continuum— for example, the range of academic performance among 11th-grade students. Extreme cases are those selected for study at either end of the continuum—in this case, 11th-grade dropouts versus those who win academic awards. Studies of geniuses, psychopaths, musical child prodigies, or Nobel Prize winners are extreme case studies.

Definition: Extreme cases are those representing the ends of a defined population continuum

Definition:
Typical case selection involves selection based on a known average for the population

Definition:
Unique case selection means selecting for study a nonreplicable event or situation

Definition:
Reputational case selection involves the selection of a study group based on recommendations by experts

Definition:
Ideal case selection involves choosing a case because it possesses all of the necessary components for program success or maximum presence of characteristics of interest to the researcher

Definition:
Comparable case selection refers to choosing cases because of their similarity to central characteristics of interest to researchers

Cross Reference:
See Book 4, Chapter 1 on network sampling

2. **Typical case selection.** The researcher finds the mean or average set of characteristics of a population and then locates subjects to study who match the mean portrait. Studies of the average housewife, teacher, factory worker, chat group, or diabetic exemplify typical case studies. Typical case selection requires that the population already be well enough known that a mean or average can be identified.

3. **Unique case selection.** The researcher finds a case or event set apart from the normal flow of events—and generally not replicable—and studies it. Studies of the impact of the Challenger spacecraft explosion on school children and of city dwellers' response to an earthquake, hurricane, or sudden influx of immigrants exemplify unique case studies.

4. **Reputational case selection.** Researchers solicit recommendations from experts about people who best exemplify the kind of person the researchers want to study. Studies of competent administrators, expert mechanics, trustworthy drug dealers, talented music students, or uncooperative patients can be constructed using reputational case selection.

5. **Bellwether or ideal case selection.** The researcher describes a "recipe" for a situation in which the researcher can say, "These are the ideal conditions under which to observe the phenomenon in which I am interested." The researcher then seeks out an example that matches that recipe or description. Studies of so-called effective schools are bellwether studies, as are studies of medical treatment administered under optimum conditions.

6. **Comparable case selection.** The researcher chooses cases because of their similarity along central characteristics of interest to the researcher. Cases may be independent (and randomly assigned to the treatment or comparison group); matched, as in a case-control design; or connected, as in a network study in which one person who is selected because he or she meets the study inclusion criteria, lists others he or she knows with the same characteristics, who are then included in the study. Studies that attempt to replicate the findings of a previous study in a similar site or with a similar population often are comparable case studies. Multiple-site ethnographies, where researchers are attempting to study the same phenomenon in similar settings, also involve comparable case selection.

Once researchers have identified the type of population and cases that will meet their research needs, they must determine *who* will be studied. This requires two steps: First, researchers must operationalize and bound the population to be studied, and then they must define a unit of analysis.

"Who" to Study: Defining, Operationalizing, and Bounding a Population

To obtain a population that can actually be studied, researchers must "operationally define" and then "bound" the population. In the previous section, we discussed how researchers select populations whose characteristics are of greatest interest to the researcher. Operationally defining such a population means locating a specific group that has those characteristics. For example, researchers might be interested in studying why people persist in building houses in flood-prone areas. They then either need to find a population that lives in a flood plain and wait for a flood to occur, or locate a community that has just experienced a flood and study the population there.

Bounding the population is a related process; it sometimes results in operationally defining the population to study—as in the case of the flood plain study just described. However, operationally defining a population does not always bound it. For example, a researcher interested in studying high-achieving 11th graders (an extreme case study) might operationally define the population in terms of 11th graders in a specific community but then bound the study by limiting it to 11th graders involved in the honor society at several specific schools. Similarly, researchers interested in studying psychopathic killers (another extreme case) probably cannot, or would not want to, study all known psychopathic killers, or even those who are currently incarcerated. The researcher probably could not even get access to most incarcerated psychopathic killers. However, the researcher *could* identify an organization that works with such individuals and bound the study by limiting it to those under the care of the organization. By contrast, Harry Wolcott's (1987) study of a school principal used typical case selection; Wolcott used data from the United States' National Education Association to determine the average characteristics of school principals in the United States; upon discovering that the "average" principal was a white, middle-aged, married male with a master's degree, he then asked the local school district in which he lived to assist him in finding such a person. The study was bounded, in a sense, by the number of individuals in the district who fit the description, but also by the number who were willing to let Wolcott observe them day after day for a year.

Populations can be bounded by whatever sets of criteria the researchers decide are relevant to the study. Sometimes, the population is easily defined because it is *naturally bounded*—for example, anthropologists often studied island communities whose population was limited to island residents. In drug research, naturally bounded populations can be found in locations termed "high-risk sites," such as shooting galleries and apartment buildings. Educational researchers often define their populations in terms of those students enrolled in particular subject areas, classrooms, or schools. Many applied researchers even end up investigating groups that define themselves by requesting the study. One such example is that of an organization consisting of Puerto Rican mothers of children with disabilities (the self-defined bounded population) who contacted the Institute for Community Research with a request to conduct research on the effects of advocacy on their children's access to educational resources. Researchers interested in studying behavior in and with specific ethnic or social race groups define the population by geography, ethnic identity (as determined by the individuals themselves or as ascribed by others), or both. In these instances, the group's self-definition—by national origin, tribal identity, reconstructed history, place of current residence, membership in a contemporary group, or a variety of other means—can influence how a researcher decides to bound a group.

In many cases, researchers start out wanting to investigate a problem involving a particular kind or category of person without knowing exactly who those people are or where they might be found. Sometimes, these groups are *artificially bounded,* in that they consist of people who have specific characteristics in common but either do not belong to any identifiable social group or belong to many different groups, none of whose affiliation definitively establishes group boundaries. Examples include youthful artists, unmarried pregnant teenagers, classical music lovers, and children with limited English proficiency. Others who *could* be defined as members of a group—American Indians, for example—still must be defined in terms of a location or site in which the group can be found—a reservation, urban Indian center, or Pow Wow group. People who possess still other characteristics of interest to researchers may not be easy to locate, either because the characteristics involved are illegal or stigmatized —users of illegal drugs, pedophiles, or homosexuals—or unknown to those who possess them or difficult to diagnose—as in the case of individuals infected with HIV but still asymptomatic, sufferers from Alzheimer's disease, or carriers of genetically linked disabilities such as Recombinant 8 syndrome or Huntington's chorea.

Cross Reference: See Book 4, Chapter 3 on ways to locate such hidden populations

Table 5.1 provides some examples of how populations with characteristics of interest to a researcher were operationally defined and then bounded within groups to which the researcher could obtain access.

Clearly, not everyone in the locations used for operational definition possess the characteristics defined as desired by the researchers in their search for a target population; however, such sites are more likely to be saturated with

TABLE 5.1 Identifying Population Boundaries

Population to Be Studied	Geographic/Definitional Boundaries Studied	Method of Identification
Urban Indian elementary school children	Children enrolled in Osborne school district	Identified through parents
Hispanic youth with HIV/AIDS	Members of specific gay/lesbian/bisexual adolescent support groups; attendees at the local Youth Center for Hispanic HIV Affected Teens	Identified first through adult social workers and facilitators and then through self-definition
Potential artist users of a proposed community arts center	Artists represented by local galleries; members of local crafts co-op; participants in community college arts classes	Researcher-created list of organizational memberships; self-defined artists and possible Center users
Adolescent smokers	Young people in targeted urban neighborhoods	Self-defined through door-to-door enumeration of households with adolescents who smoke
Older adults at risk of sexually transmitted diseases	Adults over 50 years of age living in geographic areas where injection drug use and unprotected sex occur	All adults over the age of 55 in buildings housing older adults in the target city

people who *do* possess such characteristics. Such saturated sites are more likely to be fruitful areas in which to do investigations. Regardless of how it is done, defining and bounding the population permits the researchers to distinguish between who or what is to be included or excluded in the population. Those to be included in the study are the "units" to be studied.

Definition:
A unit of analysis is the element that will be studied and used as the basis of comparison in the analysis of the study data

What Is a Unit of Analysis?

Simply put, researchers call the specific "things" they study **units of analysis.** Usually, in social science research, the unit under study is a person—or a group of people. For example, in a study of voting behavior, each voter is a unit of analysis. However, units of analysis can be many other things: cities, families, corporations, states, school districts, health care agencies, time periods, paragraphs in written texts or documents, interactions, books or novels, and clauses in transcripts. In intervention studies or experiments, they also may be—but are not always—what experimenters call "units of intervention." These units are the individuals who participate in the treatment and control groups constituting an experiment. They could be classrooms selected for studies of the effectiveness of reading programs, groups of injection drug users participating in studies of drug use prevention programs, or high-risk sites in which youth or adults are involved in risk behaviors that could affect their health.

Characteristics, Size, and
Location of Units of Analysis

Whatever they choose as their unit, researchers need to define units of analysis in operational terms because they need to be able to identify discrete individuals (or units) from the given population for observation, questioning, and/or counting. Here are some simple rules for defining units of analysis:

- They must be countable.
- They must be measurable or describable.
- They must be locatable.
- Their beginnings and endings must be identifiable (i.e., the researcher must be able to distinguish clearly one unit of analysis from another).
- If the researcher is planning a survey, units of analysis also must be able to be located on a list of individuals or able to be enumerated or counted so that a list can be created and a sample drawn.

Following are some examples of how researchers defined populations and then identified appropriate units of analysis within those populations.

EXAMPLE 5.4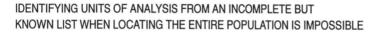

IDENTIFYING UNITS OF ANALYSIS FROM AN INCOMPLETE BUT
KNOWN LIST WHEN LOCATING THE ENTIRE POPULATION IS IMPOSSIBLE

The American Home Brewers' Association wanted to determine how often home brewers produced their beer and how much they consumed. They also wanted to know which of the Association's services were most useful. They invited a researcher to design and administer a survey to answer their questions. The population of interest was "people who brew their beer at home," but the Association did not have any way to contact every single person who might be a home brewer. Instead, the researcher decided to mail a survey to every person who subscribed to the Association's newsletter.

━●━●━

In the preceding example, the general population of interest is people who brew beer at home; for convenience, a unit of analysis from this population is defined as a person who receives a particular publication. This definition, of course, omits from the survey all of the potentially numerous people who brew beer at home but who do not subscribe to the Association's newsletter. The problem was that the Association did not have any reasonable way to contact such people, and it had to account for the potential biases stemming from this unavoidable exclusion of potential respondents by describing them in terms of limitations in the selection process.

Less simply put, many studies—especially ethnographies—involve more than one, and more than one kind of, unit of analysis. Usually, smaller scale units are embedded

within larger scale units. Below are several other examples that used several populations and a number of corresponding-ing units of analysis.

 **EXAMPLE 5.5**

IDENTIFYING MULTIPLE UNITS OF ANALYSIS IN
A STUDY OF TEACHER COMPETENCY TESTING

Shepard and Kreitzer (1987) studied what happened when the State of Texas decided to test all of its teachers for competency in reading, writing, and basic computation. The state created the TECAT (Test of Educational Competency for All Teachers), administered it to all practicing teachers, established training centers with materials to help those who failed the test succeed on subsequent attempts, and ended up firing a small percentage of teachers who never passed the examination. The researchers interviewed the politicians and businessmen who advocated the program and the legislators and policymakers who created it; analyzed newspapers, program plans, and documents; and talked to teachers who took the tests, staff at the remedial training centers, and principals at schools. They also examined the results of the TECAT itself.

 **EXAMPLE 5.6**

IDENTIFYING MULTIPLE UNITS OF ANALYSIS IN A STUDY OF TEACHER BEHAVIOR

LeCompte's (1975) study of teacher behavior in elementary schools began with a fourth-grade teacher as the unit of analysis. However, written descriptions of the teacher's behavior in the classroom yielded three other units of analysis: verbal episodes, activity segments, and minutes—either instructional, managerial, or discretionary. They constituted and were embedded within the teacher's "stream of behavior." Identifying the categories of these units and aggregating them permitted the researcher to determine the underlying structure of classroom life for this teacher and three other teachers who were similarly observed and analyzed.

The studies just described constitute good examples of research using *embedded samples,* or smaller scale and quite different units of analysis embedded within the larger unit of analysis. Each study started with one unit—in one case, a teacher, and in the other, a program. For this reason, they are considered to be *case studies.* However, the units themselves are quite complex. The TECAT program described in Example 5.5 involved many different kinds of people over a period of several years; documenting what really happened and the impact that the TECAT had on teachers required that the researchers look at a wide variety of data sources. Thus, their population of *one* program (one unit of analysis) included other populations of teachers (another kind of unit); legislators, politicians, and test administrators (other kinds of units); newspaper articles (another, different kind of unit); policy documents; archival texts and tests (more kinds of units); and many other things.

The researchers had to define *units* from each of these populations and then provide criteria for how they would identify them. For example, they identified three kinds of teachers within the general population of teachers: those who passed the test on the first try, those who passed it after one or more failed attempts, and those who never passed it. A sample from each of these categories was interviewed or sent a self-administered questionnaire to complete and return to the researchers.[2]

Even a unit apparently less complex than a statewide program can yield many different populations. The behavior of LeCompte's four teachers in Example 5.6 was made up of populations of activity segments and verbal episodes; these, in turn, took place over a population of minutes—which varied, in turn, by the type of activity. These units had to be operationally defined, just as the home brewers and the teachers were, in order for the researcher to make decisions about what would and would not be included in the category—or where one unit began and another left off.

For example, LeCompte defined a verbal episode as the words, gestures, and pauses included between the initiation of a topic and its end. Thus, verbal episodes varied considerably in duration, but they were distinguishable from one another because each one addressed a single identifiable topic.

Defining units of analysis is relatively easy to do when the units are discrete, as in the case of people or organizations; people usually are limited by their physical characteristics—or, as in the case of the TECAT, by actions they do or do not take—and organizations are limited by their members. However, the boundaries of people and organizations can blur depending upon the way they are defined and the purposes for which they are being studied. In a study of role behavior, for example, when does an employed woman obstetrician with children cease being a mother and start being a doctor? And when is she a friend—and neither a doctor nor a mother? Even what might seem to be unambiguous physiological characteristics can blur: Suppose a researcher wanted to study the health-related behavior of "women of childbearing age." Census data and other demographic studies often define such a population operationally as "all females between the ages of 15 and 50." However, although such a definition probably maximizes the number of units with the desired physiological characteristic—fertility—it also includes many females who cannot, will not, or do not have children, for one reason or another. It also eliminates females above age 50 and below age 15 who are capable of having children. Thus, researchers can either elicit the help of the women (the research participants in the study) in order to make specific and proper distinctions among individuals in a general population, or risk obtaining data that are rendered somewhat inaccurate because they include units of analysis that are inappropriate to the study.

Researchers can clarify the characteristics of individuals by carefully worded initial questions in surveys or by careful preliminary fieldwork that permits identification in advance of a population limited to individuals whom the researchers really want to investigate.

Enumerating, Choosing, and
Sampling Units of Analysis

Definition:
A sample is a systematically selected subset of a larger population

Definition of units of analysis occurs prior to and is critical to the process of creating a **sample**. Researchers (and laypeople, too!) sometimes use the term *sample* instead of *population* to refer to the group under study; however, this is, strictly speaking, inaccurate. Representative samples are used when studying the entire population of interest is too time-consuming or expensive, or when it is not realistic because the population is too large. Under these conditions, researchers create samples by systematically choosing (sampling) members from the population in such a way that the smaller group accurately represents the larger one. Samples, however, cannot be created from groups whose size and characteristics are not already known fairly well in advance. This is because researchers must make their selection of a sample by accurately choosing some representatives from each of the many different types of members in the group or population. If the researcher does not know what types of members are included in the group, it is impossible to create a sample that is representative. However, if the types included in the group are already broadly known, then "quota sampling," the simplest form of sampling, is appropriate.

Quota sampling. Quota sampling involves deciding how many subgroups there might be within the population of interest and then selecting a set number of individuals (a quota) of people from each of these subgroups. For example, political analysts might have determined that 50% of the population in a particular census tract was white, 30% was African American, and 20% was Latino, and that women were as likely to vote as men. To predict which candidate that census tract would choose in an election, they could interview 100 voters—50 males and 50 females —as they exited from the polling places, dividing them according to what the researchers thought their ethnicity was and asking them how they voted. Wanting to interview 50 whites, 30 African Americans, and 20 Latinos, they would first determine their respondents' ethnicity by asking them to identify themselves, and then they would interview until they had filled their quota of each ethnic group. If they had already interviewed 25 male and 25 female whites, they would try to avoid questioning anyone who looked white and would exclude from interviewing anyone who identified as white despite the researcher's previous attempt at identification. Quota sampling, however, is not a very accurate way to represent the characteristics of a group.

Systematic and probabilistic sampling. More accurate methods for selection involve systematic or probabilistic sampling. These strategies require the compilation of a comprehensive list of all of the members of the given population. Such a list ensures that all members have a chance to be included in the sample, and it permits the researcher to check to see that the sample drawn really is representative— that is, that it does possess the same characteristics as the larger population. It also permits researchers to accurately assess how big the group really is, and, therefore, what percentage of the population should end up being sampled.

To initiate the sampling process, researchers first define the units of analysis. Then they find or create a list of the specific units to be contacted for the study, or they find, enumerate, and list the units from within a population of inanimate objects, such as books, documents, artifacts, or time segments. Once the list is created, its characteristics are scrutinized once again, and then mathematical procedures are used to select a representative sample of a size that the researchers can reasonably manage to study, given their resources. For more information on the sampling process, see Book 2 of this series, or any number of books on sampling procedures (e.g., Henry, 1990; also see Bernard, 1995, for a discussion of sampling related to ethnography).

NOTES

1. In fact, it could be argued that *no* contemporary group on the globe is isolated in the manner assumed by traditional anthropology.

2. A unit of analysis also can be a *sampling* unit when, as in the case of Shepard and Kreitzer's study, it defines what kinds of items will be selected from a larger population.

COLLECTING ETHNOGRAPHIC DATA

DATA COLLECTION TECHNIQUES

Books 2, 3, and 4 of the **Ethnographer's Toolkit** specify in detail the methods and data collection techniques that researchers use for collecting their data. Table 6.1 provides a general overview and summary of the general strategies used by ethnographic researchers, the purposes for each strategy, the target populations for which the strategies are best suited, and what the data look like once they are collected. Book 2 covers what we have termed the "essential methods" of ethnography: observation, tests and repeated measures, surveys, interviews, and content analysis. Essential methods, especially participatory observation and interviews, are those without which no researcher can conduct an ethnography. Book 3 addresses several important supplementary or "enhanced" data collection strategies: focus group interviews, audio- and videotaping, and elicitation techniques. These are commonly used in ethnographies, but we call them enhanced techniques because they are used to enhance or make more rigorous a study that is already set up as an ethnography. By themselves, they cannot be used to create such a study. Book 4 addresses three rather specialized forms of data collection, analysis, and

TABLE 6.1 Data Collection Methods

Method	Purpose	Target	Procedures for Data Collection	Data Content
Observation	— Record situations as they happen — Record the meanings of these events at the time for study group participants	— Activities — Events and sequences — Settings, participation structures — Behaviors of people and groups — Conversations — Interactions	— Written or taped fieldnotes — Written or taped records of informal interviews and conversations — Video records — Photographs — Maps — Observational checklists	— Depiction of: • Physical settings • Acts • Activities • Interaction patterns • Meanings • Beliefs • Emotions
Tests and repeated measures	— Determine efficacy of an intervention or verify a hypothesis about a treatment or innovation	— Intervention — Innovative program or treatment	— Systematic observations or survey data collected at two or more points in time	— Qualitative or quantitative measures of change from Time 1 to Time 2 (and beyond)
Population or sample survey	— Determine variation in attitudes, knowledge, perceptions, demographic information, and behavior of study population — Obtain limited information from many people	— A large group — A representative sample drawn from a large group	— Self-administered questionnaires — Structured interviews	— Quantifiable answers to closed-ended and forced choice or multiple choice questions
Ethnographic interview	— In-depth information on selected topics — Personal histories — Cultural knowledge and beliefs — Description of practices	— Representative individuals — Key informants or topic experts	— In-depth interviews: • Unstructured • Semistructured • Elicitation techniques (including vignettes or dilemmas)	— Answers to open-ended questions — Responses to elicitation materials

Method	Purpose	Target	Procedures for Data Collection	Data Content
Content analysis of secondary text or visual data	— Elicitation of themes or content in a body of written or visual media	— Documents — Artifacts — Artistic products — Transcripts — Photographic or videotaped records	— Repeated observation — Development of analytic categories — Coding — Enumeration	— Coded or sorted text or visual media
Focus group interviews	— Obtain information about: • Norms • Behaviors • Attitudes • Cultural domains • Innovations • Instrument content	— Target groups familiar with or belonging to the phenomenon or group under study	— Interviewer-led group discussion — Interviewer use of group elicitation techniques	— Transcripts of conversations guided by the interviewer's questions and text coded
Elicitation methods	— Obtain data on ways that people categorize and organize understanding of cultural domains using stimuli	— Individuals — Small, representative sample(s) of people from the target group or groups	— Interviewer requests individual responses to elicitation tools (pictures, maps, lists, material items)	— Lists — Sorted or categorized items — Transcripts of discussions
Audiovisual methods	— Obtain accurate audio or visual record of events, interviews, and program activities	— Key informants — Groups with expertise in research topic — Small groups or classrooms — Special events	— Targeted taped or camera-recorded events or components of events selected in advance	— Coded transcripts of audiotapes and videotapes
Spatial mapping	— Obtain data on the ways in which cultural data vary across spatial units	— Representative samples of target group, institutions, or material culture	— Individual and group interviews on cultural variables and their location in space — Observations of the location of events, institutions, and material culture	— Geocoded responses to surveys — Counts of use — Spatially located qualitative or quantitative units for mapping

(continued)

TABLE 6.1 Continued

Method	Purpose	Target	Procedures for Data Collection	Data Content
Network research	— Obtain data on patterns of relationships and exchanges among individuals, groups, and other social units — Understand diffusion of behavior and information through a network	— Representative, targeted, snowball, or systematic network sample of the target population	— Interviews with index (startpoint) individuals and members of their networks	— Quantified behavioral, attitudinal, or knowledge-based variables for individuals and their contacts, pairs (dyads), and larger groups — Qualitative description of networks in space and time

Cross Reference: See Book 4 for information on these topics

sampling used by ethnographers for specific purposes. These are social network analysis, spatial mapping, and the location and selection of so-called hidden populations, whose characteristics we outlined in Chapter 5.

Any of the above-listed data collection strategies could be used alone in a perfectly viable qualitative study, but by themselves, most could not create an ethnography. This is because doing ethnography requires reconstruction of the cultural characteristics of the people or groups under study; doing so is a complex process that requires multiple sources of data, each of which is used to confirm the accuracy of the others.

Using Multiple or Alternative Sources of Data: Triangulation and Redundancy

Just as aeronautical and civil engineers build mechanical and structural redundancy into airplanes and bridges, ethnographic researchers build redundancy into their data collection methods. This is done for several reasons. First, multiple sources of data serve as sources of confirmation or corroboration for each other. Just as surveyors never establish the existence of a straight line with fewer than three points, researchers try to ensure that each question asked is answered by more than one data source. This is not merely duplication of effort; instead, it ensures that information elicited from each key informant is corroborated by information from others—preferably people who have different perspectives on the subject or who occupy different positions in the project from initial informants. For example, data collected from documents such as project proposals and organizational charts are verified or cross-checked by field observations or interviews with participants; or assertions made about an issue or event by key informants are matched against information about the same topics from a sample survey of the entire population under study. Another reason for using multiple sources of data is to make sure that if one data set or source proves to be unreliable or incomplete, others will suffice to provide the information needed to answer each research question posed.

Researchers call the process of creating redundancy, tri-angulation (Denzin, 1978). In The Learning Circle program, LeCompte and her team of researchers had to create redundancy in achievement data because the achievement tests mandated by the State of Arizona changed each year of the program.

Definition: Triangulation involves confirming or cross-checking the accuracy of data obtained from one source with data collected from other, different sources

EXAMPLE 6.1

TRIANGULATING STUDENT ACHIEVEMENT MEASURES TO COMPENSATE
FOR GAPS IN THE TESTING PROGRAM: THE LEARNING CIRCLE

During The Learning Circle's first 2 years, the school district in which the program was located used the Arizona Standardized Assessment Program (ASAP), a test of reading, writing, and mathematics for Grades 4 and 8. Teachers also administered a practice ASAP to Grade 3. Chapter 1 remedial programs used the federally mandated Gates-McGinitie tests to measure the impact of those programs in reading and math for students in Grades 1-6 who were enrolled in those programs. All teachers did reading inventories: criterion-referenced assessments mapped to the reading curriculum in the district. Unfortunately, none of these tests used the same scoring techniques or reporting procedures, and because no children were involved in all of the programs or grades in which tests were used, there was no systematic way to measure progress with the same instrument each year. The researchers also learned that students who were considered limited in their English proficiency had been excluded from all standardized testing. Many of these children were in programs whose enrollments could have served as comparison groups to the Learning Circle children.

In the third year of the program, the state stopped using the ASAP. Furthermore, teachers in the third school to join the program failed to administer the reading inventory to their students. Adding to all of the above problems was the high turnover of students in the district, which meant that it was difficult to find a group of children who had been enrolled in the program for more than 2 years. For the researchers, this was an assessment nightmare.

The researchers decided to do the best they could by collecting every bit of data available. First, they decided to add teacher grades as a measure of achievement and to attempt to find them for the previous years, because those measures, however subjective they might be, were the only consistently collected data on all children for all years. (Even grades were a bit of a problem; some teachers used two scales: a regular one for children in regular classes, and another, "inflated" one for children in remedial classes. An "A" in the remedial classes really counted as a "C.") They also included in the assessment the systematic collection of teacher, counselor, and parent opinions about the behavior of Learning Circle students. By *triangulating* with data from all of these sources, the researchers hoped to get a picture of how effective the program really was.

➤•➤•➤

Another example taken from ethnographic research on AIDS risk on the Island of Mauritius in the Indian Ocean shows how multiple sources of data can be integrated to provide a comprehensive picture of AIDS risk in a location where AIDS cases are rare.

EXAMPLE 6.2

TRIANGULATING DATA ON HIV RISK, DRUG USE,
AND SEXUAL BEHAVIOR IN MAURITIUS

Anthropologists Jean Schensul and Stephen Schensul, family planning director Geeta Oodit, and staff of the Mauritius Family Planning Association conducted a study of exposure to HIV infection among young adults through unprotected sexual activity. Sexual behaviors were not commonly discussed in Mauritius, especially among young, unmarried women, who considered the maintenance of virginity to be a priority. To learn about sex behaviors, the research team used a combination of data collection techniques designed to be complementary. First, young health educators conducted observations in parks, at clubs, on the beaches, and in other locations where young people were known to interact in groups or pairs. They also questioned key informants (taxi drivers, hotel receptionists, factory supervisors, club managers) about the social and sexual behavior of young women and men. These data were useful in providing information on whether and where sexual activities were carried out but not on who was involved or what they did.

To find out, researchers carried out open-ended interviews with young women to find out their histories of involvement with relationships, boyfriends, and their specific sexual behaviors. These data showed that young women were involved in unprotected penetrative sex but did not provide information on how much, how often, and with whom.

Finally, the research team conducted a 600-person survey among young women on these topics. Data from in-depth interviews provided more information on types of unprotected sexual behaviors that could be considered risky, as well as the distribution of these behaviors in the target population. Data from the survey provided information on the distribution of these risky behaviors. Data from the observations and ethnographic interviews were triangulated with survey data to provide a comprehensive picture of the changing context of sexual behaviors and increasing AIDS risk in Mauritius (Schensul, S., et al., 1994).

Both of these examples show how researchers designed studies with multiple data sources and then used each piece of information to cast light on the others. Sometimes, such triangulation actually casts doubt on the accuracy of information; usually, it permits the researcher to modify, elaborate, confirm, or adapt his or her interpretations of the cultural scene in an ongoing, recursive manner.

Although creating redundancy and triangulating with many data sources tends to produce more credible research results, a researcher's capacity to collect mountains of corroboratory data is limited by the resources available to carry out the study. In the next section, we discuss just how researchers design studies within the limits of a variety of constraints.

RESOURCE LOGISTICS

How Ethnographers Allocate Time, Money, and Staff

We have discussed previously how the size and proximity of the population or site to be studied create logistical decision points for the researcher, and in Figure 5.1, we organized some of those decisions in the form of questions that researchers must consider. Up to this point, however, we have been discussing set-up and execution of a project with little reference to the realities of resources available to the investigators. We now turn to this most important set of considerations. Generally, a researcher's resources include the following:

- Time
- Money
- Availability of a variety of skilled field-workers

- Secretarial and clerical staff
- Data managers and analysts
- Supplies and materials for data collection and analysis
- A range of requisite hard- and software, including computers, fax machines, copiers, printers, audio- and videotape recorders, and electronic communications

More or fewer of these resources will be required, depending upon the size and complexity of the topic or program under consideration; the number of sites to be included; and the time lines and informational requirements of funders, research partners, or policymakers who have an interest in the research.

Early in this book, we discussed the importance of research design in helping researchers make decisions about how they should carry out a project. Research designs should always be framed in the context of available resources so that they can guide researchers to establish the limits of what they can and should do in any given project. Clearly, to the extent possible, such limits should be negotiated in advance of the study among researchers, funders, partners in the study, and agencies commissioning or supporting the research itself. A project is of little use, no matter how impeccably done, if the results arrive long after the date by which users needed them for program planning or other deadlines. Similarly, an elegantly conceived research design that costs more than the funding agency is willing to provide will not be carried out. Most often, however, programs or research partners would like to have more information than researchers are able to provide, given the available resources. It is at this point that ingenuity is required in design so that researchers can figure out alternative—and less costly—ways to meet everyone's needs as much as possible.

EXAMPLE 6.3

NEGOTIATING LESS COSTLY STUDENT IMPACT
MEASURES FOR AN ARTS EDUCATION PROGRAM

Researchers evaluating an experimental arts program were asked to use assessments of student progress that measured the distinctly different academic content of the instruction because school personnel deemed existing achievement batteries to be inadequate. Such assessments did not exist; although some research was being carried out on the relationship between arts and cognition/achievement, it would not produce any usable instruments by the time they would be needed for the evaluation study. In addition, there were no funds to purchase such instruments even if they had been available. However, the teachers had decided to require students to keep journals about their thought processes during the program and to assemble portfolios of their work. The researchers decided to help the teachers develop strategies for coding these already legitimated student products for indicators of growth and development and then to use those indicators to assess the impact of the program.

As Example 6.3 indicates, researchers often can find sources of data that will satisfy client needs but still meet researcher needs for containing cost or meeting time lines. Following is a different sort of example in which the funder did not provide enough money to complete a study with a very broad base of community support. To meet the expectations of both the community and the funder, the organization decided to draw upon other available resources as needed. The result was a good product, delivered in a timely manner, with excellent community cooperation, but one that cost several times the amount allocated by the funder.

➡•➡•➡ **EXAMPLE 6.4**

WHEN TO JUSTIFY EXCEEDING BUDGET LIMITS ON A RESEARCH PROJECT

Community organizations, both formal and informal, were forced to react to infrastructural and service changes planned by central authorities in Connecticut cities. To assist in planning for these changes, the Institute for Community Research initiated a communitywide, neighborhood-based, participatory survey with an ethnographic component. More than 80 community organizations and 250 people participated in this project. Components included the following:

- A network of agencies that were key sources of planning and other information for their constituencies

- A census-like survey instrument prepared by experts with collaboration and critique of census questions from community and agency representatives, and administered to 2,600 households

- Focus groups and discussions in target neighborhoods that designated specific issues or problems to be explored in a separate set of open- and closed-ended questions

- Development of neighborhood histories and the creation of booklets integrating ethnographic, historical, census, and special issue data for each neighborhood

- A complete, easy-to-use data set with instructions for each of the "umbrella" agencies to use for proactive planning purposes

The primary funder, a local community foundation, provided the largest grant it had ever made to support this project. All audiences needed, and some demanded, a level of methodological sophistication and rigor comparable to that provided by much larger survey research consulting firms. Despite the level of funding provided by the foundation, the study cost approximately twice as much as the grant to support it. To cover the many unanticipated costs that arose with a study of this scope, the Institute for Community Research drew on its reserves with the full agreement of the board of directors. The result was a project and a set of products that satisfied most audiences and preserved the Institute's reputation as a community partner that met its obligations in spite of cost overruns. The materials and the model for the project are still used, 10 years later, for instructional and comparative purposes, even though the census data are now long out of date.

The entire process of matching logistics to research needs and desires can be greatly facilitated by the use of a data collection matrix that spells out the principal issues addressed in a research design.

Components of a Data Collection Matrix

1. Which research questions are to be asked
2. Which data will answer those questions
3. Where, and from whom, those data can be obtained
4. In what form the data will be collected
5. Who will be responsible for collecting, analyzing, and writing up the data
6. When each stage of data collection, analysis, and report writing will begin and end
7. How, by whom, and to whom results will be disseminated

Table 6.2 is an example of a data collection matrix that was created for one part of The Learning Circle research project. Notice that it is lacking a dissemination plan; this was developed in the context of another part of the research project.

Table 6.2 was constructed with the help of a series of questions that can be displayed—and answered—in a data planning worksheet such as that depicted in Figure 6.1. Once constructed, data matrices can be transformed into schedules and time lines such as Figure 6.2, which gives a time line and duty schedule for a 2-year study of The Learning Circle. Such planning documents permit the researcher to determine just what needs to be done, when, and by whom.

Another model is one used by the Center for Substance Abuse Prevention for demonstration research planning and evaluation purposes. As a project management tool, it uses the concept of the "GOAMs" (goals, objectives, activities,

(text continues on page 144)

TABLE 6.2 Data Collection Matrix

Research Questions	Process Data and Outcome Measures	Sources of Data
1. What are the characteristics and culture of each of the Learning Circle models?	— Cultural characteristic matrices detailing beliefs, practices, activities, and language usage in the two Learning Circle models	— Previous evaluation reports — Fieldnotes from participant and nonparticipant observation — Curriculum guides and documents — Interviews with teachers and students
2. Which processes were used to develop the alternative Learning Circle models?	— Documentation of curriculum development and program implementation	— Minutes of program staff meetings — Interviews with Learning Circle staff and Program Director
3. What adaptations to the original model were necessary for Learning Circle to work with groups other than American Indians?	— Documentation of curriculum development and program implementation	— Interviews with teachers/ parents — Interviews with community participants representing the various groups — Teacher survey instrument
4. Do children who participate in Learning Circle exhibit positive attitudes toward their own culture?	— Self-reports — Assessment of teachers/ parents — Attitude inventory	— Interviews with children — Narrative accounts of their experiences — Learning Circle anecdotal record analysis — Interviews with teachers/ parents
5. What attitudes toward people/peers from different ethnic/racial groups do Learning Circle children exhibit initially?	— Self-reports	— Attitude assessment instrument — Interviews with children
6. Do attitudes toward other ethnic/racial groups change as a consequence of participation in the program?	— Self-reports — Assessments of teachers and parents — Sociometric analyses	— Attitudinal inventory — Pretest-posttest data — Interviews with children, teachers, and parents
7. What is the nature of the intergroup interaction and interrelationships among Learning Circle and non-Learning Circle children?	— Self-reports — Assessments of teachers and parents — Sociometric analyses	— Interviews with children — Interviews with teachers and parents —Observation of children in various social settings

(continued)

TABLE 6.2 Continued

Research Questions	Process Data and Outcome Measures	Sources of Data
8. Does Learning Circle participation increase interaction among children of different ethnic/racial groups?	— Friendship matrices — Documenting inter- and cross-group conversations — Study and play groups, friendship patterns, visiting and neighboring	— Fieldnotes from participant and nonparticipant observation in various school and neighborhood settings — Classrooms, playground, hallways, lunchrooms, buses, field trips — Sociometric analysis of friendships and conversations
9. What obstacles to inter-group interactions and understanding do Learning Circle children experience in schools and community and in the program itself?	— Self-reports — Assessments of teachers/ parents/community activities and events	— Interviews with children — Narratives/stories of children's school and community experiences
10. Which Learning Circle practices, activities, and services have been most effective in fostering inter-group interaction and understanding of other ethnic groups?	— Self-reports — Attitudinal inventory — Documentation of inter- and cross-group conversations	— Interviews with children, teachers, and parents — Narratives/stories of children's school and community experiences — Fieldnotes; participant and nonparticipant observation
11. Which Learning Circle practices, activities, and services have been most effective in promoting cultural identity and self-esteem?	— Self-reports — Documentation of children's/parents' sense of cultural identity	— Interviews with children — Interviews with teachers/parents
12. Do children who participate in Learning Circle exhibit positive attitudes toward school?	— Self-reports — Assessment of teachers/ parents — Persistence in school	— Interviews with children — Interviews with teachers/parents
13. Which Learning Circle practices, activities, and services have been most effective in promoting academic success?	— Self-reports	— Interviews with children — Interviews with teachers/parents — Attendance records — Narratives/stories of children's school experiences
14. Do children who partici-pate in Learning Circle maintain satisfactory academic progress?	— Academic achievement measures	— Teacher-assigned grades — District-administered standardized test scores — Learning Circle anecdotal record analysis

What do I need to know?	Why do I need to know this?	What kind of data will answer the question?	Where can I find the data?	Whom do I contact for access?	Time lines for acquisition

Figure 6.1. Data planning worksheet.

Figure 6.2a. A project time line.

Work plan/Time line description	First-year time line: July 1996–June 1997												A
	July	Aug.	Sept.	Oct.	Nov.	Dec.	Jan.	Feb.	Mar.	Apr.	May	June	July
Time line indicating duties and responsibilities for research assistants (GRA, RA); pilot teacher (PT); program director (PD); co-principal investigator (PI); and typist													
Process Data													
– Documentation of planning and implementation of Hispanic Learning Circle Program and multicultural program (site visits/interviews/participatory observation by GRA, RA, and PI); continued monitoring of other Learning Circle sites	GRA		PI	GRA	PI		GRA	PI	GRA		PI	GRA	
Product Data													
– Collect and tabulate achievement/attendance data for children for 1995-1996	GRA												
– Collect and tabulate Learning Circle developmental records for 1995-1996	GRA												
– Baseline administration of self-esteem inventory and attitudes toward other racial groups inventory; GROB game		GRA											
Programmatic Activities													
– Planning activities and program development of the new Hispanic Learning Circle and Multicultural Learning Circle component	PT & PD												
– Ongoing curriculum development, activities, and strategies for Hispanic and Multicultural Learning Circle pilot			Program Director & Learning Circle Teachers										
– Reevaluation and modification of Hispanic Learning Circle; ongoing development of multicultural component												PT & PD	
– Linking Hispanic and Native American models with multicultural component						Program Director & Learning Circle Teachers							

142

First-year time line: July 1997–June 1998   **B**

Work plan/Time line description	July	Aug.	Sept.	Oct.	Nov.	Dec.	Jan.	Feb.	Mar.	April	May	June	July
Time line indicating duties and responsibilities for research assistants (GRA, RA); pilot teacher (PT); program director (PD); co-principal investigator (PI); and typist													
Process Data													
— Collect and tabulate achievement/attendance data for children for 1996-1997	GRA & RA	← →											
— Collect and tabulate Learning Circle developmental records for 1996-1997	GRA & RA	← →											
— Administer self-esteem inventory, attitudes toward other racial groups inventory, and intercultural interaction inventory to new Learning Circle students			GRA ↕								GRA ↕		GRA ↕
— Documentation of planning and implementation of Hispanic Learning Circle Program and multicultural program (site visits/interviews/participatory observation by GRA, RA, and PI); continued monitoring of other Learning Circle sites				GRA, RA, & PI ← →					PI & RA ← →				
Product Data													
— Collect and tabulate achievement/attendance data for children for 1997-1998											GRA ↕	GRA & RA	← →
— Administer posttest self-esteem inventory and attitudes toward other racial groups inventory; intercultural inventory											GRA & PI ↕	GRA, RA, & PI	← →
Programmatic Activities													
— Planning activities and program development of the new Hispanic Learning Circle and multicultural component	PD & LC Teachers	← →											
— Ongoing curriculum development, activities, and strategies for Hispanic and Multicultural Learning Circle pilot		←				Program Director & Learning Circle Teachers						→	
— Reevaluation and modification of Hispanic Learning Circle and multicultural component		←				Program Director & Learning Circle Teachers						→	
— Linking of Learning Circle program models and multicultural component											PD & LC Teachers	← →	

Figure 6.2b. A project time line.

143

resource allocation plan that, together with a more detailed description of the steps required to carry out the project, provide a "management by objectives" guide to the work-flow for each year of a project. These GOAMs can be moni-tored and can be changed to accommodate the realities of a project or study in the field. Furthermore, if certain critical activities are not completed within the time period desig-nated in the GOAMs, the project management is alerted to the possibility that the goal or objective might need to change, or that the project is behind and will not accomplish its designated plan in the appropriate period of time. Even a modest research project should incorporate these tools of practice as guideposts to successful implementation and completion.

Summary

In this chapter, we have reviewed the major tools for data collection from which ethnographic researchers can choose, and the circumstances under which they may prefer one set of tools over another. Usually, researchers will select at least three or four ways of collecting data because these access different kinds of information from different sub-groups within the study site. At the same time, triangulation of information on the same topic from different data sources is critical to the validity and reliability of ethno-graphic research. Studies that use only one means of data collection can be subject to criticism for lack of scientific rigor. We have also reminded readers of the importance of thinking through in advance what resources and logistics are required to carry out a study. Sufficient resources and careful and realistic planning can go a long way toward en-suring the success of a study, even when conditions in the field change.

Goal 1: To decrease (and delay) the incidence of ATOD use among female adolescents by:
(a) identifying and specifying methods to reduce factors in the individual, family, and significant others, school, peer group, neighborhood/community, and society/media that increase young women's vulnerability to initiating ATOD use; and
(b) enhancing factors in the individual, family and significant others, school, peer group, neighborhood/community, and society/media that strengthen young women's resiliency and protect them against alcohol, tobacco and other drugs.

Objective 1: To build a social structural alternative to ATOD use and other risky behavior for young women aged 11-15 and their female caregivers from the three targeted neighborhoods by developing and strengthening multi-ethnic positive peer clusters.

Interventions: Bi-weekly (girls) and weekly (women) curriculum meetings

Plans to Measure:
1. Ethnographic documentation of program process, focus on facilitation techniques, group response, and content of intervention sessions.
2. Increase in program friendships and peer intimacy and reduction in risk-involved peer pressure (daughter) using the *Peer Risk Ratio* (with a subsample). J. Schensul and P. Weeks and the *Peer Intimacy and Social Influences and Expectations subscales from EMT ATOD Youth Survey of national cross-site evaluation.*
2. Repeated measures, pre- and 3 post- program 6 month follow-ups with treatment and comparison groups *Using EMT ATOD Youth Survey of national cross-site evaluation; Multi-group Ethnicity Measure; Parent/Adolescent Communication Scale; Mother/Daughter Relationship Scale; Culture free self-esteem inventory; and HIV/AIDS & Relationships Survey (girls only).*

Activities	Target Dates	Actual Completion	Comments
EXAMPLES OF ADMINISTRATIVE ACTIVITIES			
A7 Recruit and Hire Staff			
A1.1 Advertise for Director and trainers	10/15/94	10/15/94	
A1.2 Interview for Director	11/1/94-11/15/94	11/1/94-11/15/94	
A1.3 Hire Director	11/18/94	11/18/94	
A1.4 Interview trainers	11/20/94-12/5/94	11/20/94-12/5/94	
A1.10 Hire trainers	2/15/95	2/17/95	
A1.11 One trainer left project	2/5/96		Personal/target population shift
A1.14 Hire Outreach Tracker	2/20/96		To recruit/retain control group
A6 Develop Pilot Program			
A6.1 Begin recruiting for pilot program	6/1/95	7/15/95	
A6.2 Orientation Session	7/5/95-7/5/95	7/7/95, 7/6/95	
A6.3 Curriculum Sessions	7/10/95-8/7/95	7/10/95-8/7/95	
A6.4 Assessment of Pilot	8/14/95	8/14/95	
EXAMPLES OF PROGRAM ACTIVITIES			
P1 Develop Pilot Program			
P1.1 Begin recruiting for pilot program	6/1/95	7/20/95	
P1.2 Orientation Session	7/5/95-7/7/95	7/5/95-7/6/95	
P1.3 Curriculum Sessions	7/10/95-8/7/95	7/10/95-8/7/95	
P1.4 Assessment of Pilot	8/14/95	8/14/95-8/15/95	

Figure 6.3. Example of management model, using Goals, Objectives, Activities, and Management Plan (GOAMs)[a].

a. These materials are excerpts from the project titled "Urban Women Against Substance Abuse," a 5-year substance abuse prevention and education program funded by the National Center for Substance Abuse Prevention.

The next step in research design is considering ways in which ethnographic data can be analyzed and triangulated to produce answers to research questions, and the research "story." In Chapter 7, we provide a language and set of procedures for approaching the initially daunting task of ethnographic data analysis.

7 ━●━◆━●━

DATA ANALYSIS: HOW ETHNOGRAPHERS MAKE SENSE OF THEIR DATA

The data collection process can be exhilarating because of the excitement of discovery and the pleasure of interacting with and enjoying the process of learning from participants in the study. The process of analyzing data, by contrast, may seem daunting at first as researchers face unanalyzed piles of data. At the same time, it can be as exhilarating as data collection, because analysis permits researchers to make sense of what they have learned. What is especially exciting and satisfying about ethnographic data analysis is that the process is recursive or iterative; that is, interpretation begins with the first steps into the field; the first set of fieldnotes and experiences; and the first set of guesses, hunches, or hypotheses. It continues until a fully developed and well-supported interpretation emerges, ready to be communicated to others.

Data analysis means figuring out what to do with the mountains of data that ethnographic research projects generate—drawers full of fieldnotes; boxes of interviews and tests; stacks of documents, maps, logs, artifacts, drawings, and charts; photographs; video- and audiotapes; survey data; and other kinds of materials. All of these must be

Cross Reference: See Book 5 for how ethnographers put the "story" together

organized, sorted, coded, reduced, and patterned into a "story" or interpretation that responds to the questions that guided the study in the first place and that is sufficiently coherent and comprehensible so that it can be communicated to a variety of audiences. Some of this sorting, organizing, and coding occurs throughout the life of the study; much of it happens toward the end as most of the questions are answered and the moment approaches for putting the whole picture together.

ANALYSIS AS A COGNITIVE PROCESS AND A TECHNICAL PROCEDURE

Most people who have had classes in statistics remember that such courses treat analysis as a technical or mathematical procedure. Having collected their data, researchers enter them into a computer, which performs a number of mathematical manipulations and then emits finished results—graphs, tables, percentages, and levels of significance. These manipulations are guided by an already established theoretical approach, a predetermined set of instruments, and a blueprint for analysis, although there may be plenty of room for exploration in quantitative analysis as well.

In ethnographic research, some raw data—numerical test scores, for example—*can* be entered directly into a computer and statistically manipulated. Most ethnographic raw data, however, arrive on the desk of researchers as piles of open-ended or semistructured questionnaires, field-notes, audio- and videotapes, maps, transcripts, documents, and other memorabilia, in a form not readily amenable to quantitatively oriented, computer-based analysis. In fact, for many kinds of ethnographic analysis, computers are not necessary at all. Therefore, we begin our discussion of analysis at a stage considerably prior to any encounter with a computer—as raw data is received.

Cross Reference: See Books 2 and 5 for more discussion on decisions regarding computerization of qualitative text or graphic data

When Does Data Analysis Begin?

We think of analysis as beginning in the mind of the researcher as a conceptual and cognitive process. Researchers need to figure out what patterns their data can reveal and what stories their data tell. To do this, they have to sift through the piles of information and begin to make sense of them. Experimental or survey researchers begin their data analysis only after most or all of their data have been collected. By contrast, ethnographers begin data analysis well before data collection is complete—even as early as when the first few interviews have been conducted. This is because, as the examples from Chapter 2 indicate, ethnographers often do not know very much, if anything, about what is going on in the sites they are studying. They may begin with a question; have only a general idea of what they are seeking to discover; or start with an initial, very general model representing their research problem. They may even begin their research with a very clear, theoretically driven model in which items, domains, or patterns and structures are identified in advance and where the intent of the ethnography is to confirm, clarify, expand, or disconfirm the original theoretical framework. Regardless of the starting point, ethnographers' initial knowledge of the characteristics of the population(s) under study may be quite limited. *Ethnographers need to engage in several levels of analysis as they go along, because doing so helps them to make sense of what they are observing.* The overall picture never becomes clear all at once; instead, it slowly emerges from a morass of observations, interviews, and other kinds of information.

In addition, the process of getting into the field and meeting the individuals under study often raises questions that were not anticipated when the project was originally designed. These new questions may call for other, unanticipated forms of data collection and analysis that must be developed, tested, and used during the life of the study.

Cross Reference:
See Book 2, Chapters 2 and 3, for approaches to building theoretical models

Key point

Ethnographers sometimes speak of how patterns and results "emerge" from qualitative data, as if the emergence were a kind of mystical process. Although it might seem to be surrounded in a kind of mysterious haze, patterns actually emerge because the researcher is engaged in a systematic cognitive process that takes place in three stages. These stages may be termed "item," "pattern," and "constitutive" or "structural" analysis and can be thought of as different levels of abstraction in the process of cultural theory building.

Cross Reference:
See Book 5, Chapters 4, 5, and 7

Before researchers can produce scientifically supportable interpretations of their data, they have to isolate specific items or elements, patterns, and structures (or relationships among patterns in the data) that are related to the research questions. This helps to make sense of what would otherwise be an undifferentiated morass of information. The items, patterns, and structures in a set of text data begin to emerge and to become more elaborated or clarified only after the researcher has laboriously looked over, read repeatedly, tidied up (Romagnano, 1991), and organized the data. Items become those events, behaviors, statements, or activities that stand out because they occur often, because they are crucial to other items, because they are rare and influential, or because they are totally absent despite the researcher's expectations. Related items are organized into higher-order patterns or cultural domains/subdomains. Structural analysis involves linking or finding consistent relationships among patterns.

The identification of items often is guided by a preliminary model stemming from the study's research questions or concerns. This preliminary model—which usually includes an initial set of items, patterns, and even guesses about structures—is elaborated and refined as data are collected and organized during the study, new items are identified, and items expected to be present are not found and thus eliminated from the model. Alternatively, a model may emerge, becoming more and more elaborated throughout the life of the study. Subcomponents of the model can

Cross Reference:
Book 2 discusses the importance of initial modeling in framing data collection and initial organization of data in the analysis phase

emerge at any time during the study and are added to guide further data collection and analysis. The major domains or cultural components of interest in the model become the primary categories for organizing and coding. The subdomains and items arranged beneath them are additional subcategories that can be coded, classified, and manipulated.

The initial taxonomy or arrangement of items, patterns (domains), and structures derived from the initial model can be organized as hierarchies as illustrated in Figure 7.1. An initial coding system for a drug use study could look something like Figure 7.1, depending on how much knowledge the researcher had before beginning the study.

These initial conceptual categories are guides to observation and interviewing. They are continuously enhanced, expanded, subdivided, and enriched throughout the course of the research until, in the end, a much more elaborated system of organizing, arranging, and, eventually, coding data has emerged from the data that can be applied to the entire data set. Hypotheses that relate subdomains to one another both within and across domains can be constructed throughout the analysis, as well as at the end. These relationships can be explored qualitatively by considering their co-occurrence in the text. The greater the degree of clarity with respect to the research question, and the more experienced the investigator, the faster these categories emerge.

Cross Reference: See Book 3, Chapter 1 for a discussion of cultural domains

THE ITEM LEVEL OF ANALYSIS

The cognitive process that researchers use to isolate items—first-level building blocks in the process of data analysis—resembles the games that children play while learning to read: comparing and contrasting, looking for items that are like and unlike each other, sorting, sifting, matching, clumping together those that are alike, and separating those that are different. These processes facilitate defining each item clearly so that other researchers can proceed in the same fashion (see LeCompte & Preissle, 1993). Glaser and Strauss

DOMAIN/PATTERN — High-risk site (type of location of drug use)

SUBDOMAIN/SUBPATTERN	(1) Shooting gallery	(2) Apartment	(3) Abandoned building	(4) Enclosed alley	(5) Under bridge
ITEM	Exposure (degree of public access to the site)				
ITEM	Gatekeeper (whether someone is there to guide and enforce access)				
ITEM	Prevention items of any sort (clean needles, literature, condoms in packages, bleach kits, or evidence of such)				

DOMAIN/PATTERN — Patterns of drug use

SUBDOMAIN/SUBPATTERN	(1) Drug type	(2) Mode of ingestion	(3) Social context
ITEM	Marijuana	Sniff	Alone
ITEM	Cocaine	Inject	Friends
ITEM	Heroin	Smoke	Acquaintances
ITEM	etc.	etc.	Strangers, etc.

DOMAIN/PATTERN — Drug risk behaviors

SUBDOMAIN/SUBPATTERN	Needle sharing	Paraphernalia use (use of bleach, cotton, equipment for liquifying the raw drug)
(No items identified as yet)		

Figure 7.1. Predefined domains/patterns, subdomains, and units for use in a study of drugs and AIDS risk.

(1967) call this process one of "constant comparison," in which each item—whether identified previously or just emerging—is compared to all other items so that all can be clearly identified, **operationalized,** and distinguished one from the other.

Seeking negative instances—that is, items that are unlike or items that contest the identification of a given item—is particularly important in this process. It helps the researcher to avoid making premature judgments about the meaning or identification of an item. In the following example, we indicate how items were identified in one component of the Learning Circle Project. This stage of the process can take place only as the researcher reads his or her fieldnotes, interviews, and other data over and over again until they become deeply familiar, and finds multiple instances of what can be operationalized as the same phenomenon. Keeping a research journal during the course of the study, in which the researcher notes ideas and hunches as they arise, can be helpful in pursuing hunches, definitions, items, and concepts at any point in the analysis process. Such journals are likely to be full of ideas that can serve as the basis for analyses.

Definition: Operationalization means defining a concept concretely in such a way that it can be understood, observed, or categorized accurately by any researcher reviewing the same data or observing in the same setting

EXAMPLE 7.1

USING IDEAS AND HUNCHES IN RESEARCH JOURNALS TO
GENERATE ANALYTIC CATEGORIES FOR THE LEARNING CIRCLE STUDY

Initially, Learning Circle researchers noticed that parents were always contacted by the certified teachers who worked with their children, not by social workers, paraprofessionals, or other lower-status, nonacademic personnel. They also noticed that considerable effort was made to give the parents advance notice of visits and to provide parents with many choices in how they worked with the educational materials that the teachers left in the homes for child and parent usage. Also, parent meetings always involved a meal or refreshments—a practice denoting a significant event in American Indian culture. In addition, parents were encouraged to provide ideas for the curriculum.

━━●━━●━

These items of behavior—parent contacts by professionals, advance notices, parent choice of activities, and food served at program events—emerged *in a consistent pattern* after reading and rereading daily teacher schedules and transcripts of interviews conducted with the teachers, fieldnotes taken while accompanying teachers on home visits, and records of parent conversations made during evening parent meetings. Like most items identified in ethnographic research, these particular items did not emerge out of the air; they were congruent with the implicit goals of the program, even if they were not explicitly stated as goals. Other items—such as the congruity between American Indian cultural practices and the practices of The Learning Circle—might be congruent with overall theories that researchers have about how programs work or how the social world operates and is organized or with specific concepts important to the participants in the research project. Both items might have been noted earlier in the researcher's journal.

In this particular case, the researchers thought the items described in Example 7.1 to be significantly related to one of the overall objectives of the project—to help American Indian parents and their children build pride in their culture. Taken together, these items seemed to indicate that parents were taken seriously by the Learning Circle professionals, and that particular practices common to American Indian cultures were integrated, where possible, with Learning Circle activities. Example 7.1 shows how researchers work recursively back and forth from theories and past experiences to their data, and then back again from their data to theory and experience, to develop explanations for the events they observe.

THE PATTERN LEVEL OF ANALYSIS

Patterns consist of groups of items that fit together, express a particular theme, or constitute a predictable and consistent set of behaviors. Patterns are created using more or less the same cognitive process that one uses in assembling a jigsaw puzzle: You take a glimpse at the picture on the box, if there is one—or at the project descriptions, proposals, or overall objectives of the program; the glimpse might or might not provide clues to potential patterns. Next, you find the edge pieces and assemble as many of them as possible. Then, you try to locate chunks of pieces that fit together in a kind of pattern. Through the process of comparison, contrast, and integration, "items" are organized, associated with other items, and linked into higher-order patterns. The patterns may have emerged from prior studies or a study's theoretical framework, as in the drug and high-risk site taxonomies depicted in Figure 7.1. In this instance, the study focused on high-risk sites, and the first phase of the study was devoted to locating, describing, and documenting behavior in such sites. Eventually, after 6 months of ethnography, the field team defined high-risk sites in a way quite different from the starting position and only tangentially related to the subdomains originally designated. With the additional knowledge obtained by ethnographers and outreach workers, a high-risk site was operationalized as either public (no gatekeeper) or private. Private sites could be one of four types, with or without gatekeepers and with or without a prevention orientation.

THE CONSTITUTIVE OR STRUCTURAL LEVEL OF ANALYSIS

Gradually, as more and more chunks of patterned pieces are assembled, the entire picture comes together. The same thing occurs in a research project as the pieces of the analytic puzzle come together to create an overall picture—or to constitute the structure—of the phenomenon under investigation. Of course, with jigsaw puzzles, the underlying structure or design is determined by the manufacturer beforehand; all that the person putting it together has to do is discover what the puzzle's creators intended for the user to discover. Occasionally, however, puzzles are created that can be used in novel ways; sometimes, the pieces of a puzzle are used for collage or as part of a completely different design. In both cases, the piece is then transformed into an original work of art. Researchers also often discover things that are completely new and unanticipated in their data. Thus, although the analytic process often uses the researcher's past experiences, previous research studies, and social science theories to create the initial frameworks for defining items and patterns—or, to use the puzzle metaphor, the edge pieces that bound the overall design—these frames do not have to dictate the ultimate course that the analysis takes.

In the case of The Learning Circle, the items of parent-related behavior fit together into a pattern that the researchers came to call "Respect." The researchers were aware of the importance of *respect* both from their previous experience with Indian populations and from prior studies other researchers had done with Indians. In The Learning Circle, Indian practices, beliefs, ways of communicating, and standards for behavior were given more importance than were mainstream practices, beliefs, and standards. That importance was demonstrated in item behaviors such as those described in Example 7.1. It clearly marked differences between how American Indian teachers, children, and parents were treated in The Learning Circle and their treatment in mainstream programs. Looking farther, a pattern of program-to-parent-related behavior that took parents' status and ideas seriously—combined with similar patterns of director-to-teacher-related behavior, teacher-to-teacher-related behavior, and teacher-to-student-related behavior—seemed convincing evidence that the culture of The Learning Circle itself was structured around taking seriously the ways of knowing, behaving, believing, and acting of American Indian people. The researchers identified this overall structural element or theme as "respect," and they determined that the theme of respect was, indeed, one of the reasons why the program was so successful in inspiring participation of Indian parents and children, as well as higher achievement among the students. What was most interesting about this discovery was the fact that the concept of respect, as it was revealed in the ethnographic study, was not defined by program initiators as a goal or process central to the program. Nevertheless, parents, evaluators, and program staff felt the program was successful. By organizing observed items into patterns of behavior by director, teachers with parents, and teachers with students, the ethnographers discovered that, overall, implementation was conducted in such a way that it signaled respect for Indian culture, and they were able to suggest to program staff that "respect" was a principal reason for that success.

COMPLEX ANALYSIS WITH MULTIPLE LEVELS AND SOURCES OF DATA

Once researchers have identified items and assembled them into patterns and larger structures, they can begin to manipulate them further—ordering, scaling, and counting them and testing hypotheses by exploring their interrelationships and by creating models. However, these processes can be done only *after* discrete "things" that are orderable, scaleable, or countable have been isolated from the stream of data. These elements can be isolated early or adapted from other people's measurement instruments, and then quantified for use in computerized statistical analyses. For example, they can be formulated into scales or indexes for use in various types of correlational analyses. Alternatively, text data can be coded using larger categories such as those in the coding trees in Figure 7.1, or concepts such as "respect" in the case of the Learning Circle analysis. These coded data "chunks" can be managed by hand or through computer programs designed for the management and analysis of large amounts of text data. Regardless of how they are handled, researchers must allow considerable time for the kinds of cognitive activities described above to take place before they can engage in more sophisticated analysis. A major difference between qualitative and quantitative data analysis is that ethnographic analysis of qualitative or text data begins with the first set of observations as items; after these are aggregated into, or categorized as parts of, domains, they can then be compared, contrasted, defined, and confirmed on an ongoing basis.

Ethnographic and qualitative data are formulated and reformulated repeatedly into models consisting of relationships; these models are tested continuously against what researchers encounter in the research site. The process becomes what we refer to as iterative or recursive analysis. This process cannot begin with quantitative data until items have been clearly identified during ethnographic study; once this has occurred, a sufficient number of them can be enumerated using quantitative instruments with enough respondents to make the model-building process worthwhile. In addition, whereas qualitative analysis may begin with the first interview, we do not usually begin quantitative analysis until we have at least 50% of the sample in; even then, there is little we can declare as results because the response rate is short of representativeness.

Cross Reference: See Chapter 4, Tables 4.4 and 4.5, for a depiction of how ethnographers can use qualitative and quantitative data to supplement each other in a study; see also Book 2 for a more extended discussion of mixing types of data

Summary

When ethnographers collect both qualitative and quantitative data, the qualitative data are continuously analyzed, providing the basis for survey or other quantitative research to follow. Sometimes, the qualitative data stand alone; sometimes, they provide working hypotheses that guide the construction of the quantitative research. Qualitative data can also supplement, extend, or provide context or explanation for the quantitative data. The process of integrating qualitative and quantitative data —seeing how each analysis verifies, validates, and enhances the other—is the final form of triangulation, and it happens at the end of the analysis process. Book 5 of the **Ethnographer's Toolkit** provides a much more detailed picture of the steps in qualitative and quantitative analyses of ethnographic data and how they can be integrated to provide a complete picture of the problem or situation to be explored in the study.

8 ━◆━●━◆━●━◆

WHO SHOULD DO ETHNOGRAPHIC INVESTIGATION?

Even if all signs indicate that ethnography would be the best choice of research design, researchers need to ask, "Am I the best person to do an ethnography?" The answer may be yes, but it also may be no. Researchers have affinities for different research designs, given their particular personality, preferences, and skills. As a consequence, some researchers are not best suited to do ethnographic research. We believe that it is not sufficient for researchers simply to assess research needs at the site and decide that ethnographic research is an appropriate design. Whereas it is possible to hire someone to conduct a survey or experiment for a given research project, it is very difficult to hire someone to conduct an ethnography, because the individual hired must understand and believe in the project and be prepared to enter into the special social relations and kinds of settings required to conduct an ethnography. Even with a research team, a researcher's ability to manage an ethnographic study depends on regular and intensive involvement in the field situation. *Ethnographic research calls for long-time residence in a field setting and can require obser-*

Key point

161

vations or interviews at times that may not be convenient for researchers who require a 9-to-5 work schedule. It is also difficult to find individuals, such as students or consultants, who are able to make the time commitment required for ethnographic research unless they are paid as full-time employees.

IMPORTANT PERSONALITY AND STYLISTIC REQUISITES FOR ETHNOGRAPHERS

Whatever the setting or specific personalities may be, ethnographers must interact with people in order to understand the meaning of events and activities in the field. Ethnographers must enjoy interacting—often intensively—with large numbers of people. They also must be able to participate in the reciprocal and mutual relationships that develop in the ethnographic field site. Therefore, the ethnographer's personal style is of critical importance to his or her success as an ethnographer. Ethnographic researchers must be somewhat gregarious; shy and retiring people may feel unable to socialize freely or be uncomfortable devoting the necessary—and significant—amounts of personal time required for building relationships in a research site. The match between the person doing ethnography and the requirements of the field site also are very important; ethnographers must be able to listen once relationships are built. In fact, some field situations may call for the long-term presence of a quiet person.

Reciprocity also is important. Often, research participants will ask researchers for personal favors. Failing to respond not only harms relationships but may even jeopardize the project. Thus, ethnographers should be individuals who enjoy helping people out in difficult situations, rather than viewing such requests as an instrumental obligation encountered primarily as a means to facilitate getting data.

Ethnographic research requires investigators to be curious and inquisitive and to demonstrate these qualities by asking an endless stream of questions of research participants in both formal and informal interviewing situations. If the potential ethnographer comes from a cultural background where many topics are personal, and personal questions are never asked—especially of strangers or in public— he or she may have to practice asking questions before being able to do good ethnography. Furthermore, ethnographers may have to learn how to be wide-eyed learners. Burnett (1974) argues that ethnographers should approach learning in the field as a young child approaches learning about the world —without preconceptions and with open curiosity about everything. Such studied naïveté is not an easy stance for all researchers to adopt, yet it is critical to good ethnographic work. *If researchers act as if they know what is* **Key point** *important in the field, then research participants will be less likely to try to teach them what they need to know—and the cultural picture the researchers are trying to construct will be correspondingly less complete.*

Flexibility, lack of dogmatism, and an ability to live with ambiguity also are requisites for ethnographic research. Ethnographers often find themselves in situations where the cultural rules for behavior or ways of thinking are very different from their own. They must be able to figure out how to learn and how to apply new rules for appropriate behavior in what may seem at first to be unusual or even bizarre circumstances. It is also useful to be at least somewhat self-sufficient, because doing ethnography can be a lonely process. Ethnographers sometimes go for long periods of time at the beginnings of fieldwork without having anyone—friends, family, colleagues, or even acquaintances—with whom to share personal thoughts and ideas.

Aside from social situations, ethnographers must be able to cope with lack of structure and ambiguity in the actual practice of their work. Unlike experiments and surveys, ethnographic research designs are "emergent" rather than firmly established templates that guide a study from start to finish. That is, at the beginning of the study, the researchers may not know all of the salient research questions to be asked, and the data collection strategies anticipated initially may evolve and change in response to unexpected events or questions encountered during the study. The analytic tools of ethnography, especially those we describe in Books 2, 3, and 5, are, for the most part, intuitive. That is, unlike survey and experimental approaches to research, ethnographic analysis builds on both logical/linear and informal cognitive skills, as well as intuitive problem-solving, informal problem-solving, and information-gathering strategies we use in our everyday lives—or that we can use *only* in a limited way in the context of other information-gathering strategies we use in our everyday lives.

This apparent similarity between ethnographic processes and everyday life has led some investigators to argue that "anyone can do ethnography" in most situations. However, this is a position with which we heartily disagree. We have already argued that ethnography is not temperamentally suited to everyone, but there is a more important difference. Whereas everyday thinking and problem solving are informal and largely unconscious processes, ethnographic "theorizing"[1] and analysis involve highly disciplined, fully conscious, logical, and systematic forms of thought and information processing. Although the term may seem oxymoronic, the methods of observation, interviewing, and elicitation and the forms of intuition used so successfully by ethnographers are disciplined ones, informed by concrete strategies for "playing with ideas" and conducted with the confidence that comes from a great deal of practice. This does not mean that ordinary people cannot be trained to be ethnographic field-workers, or that one has to be born with ethnographic insights. Certainly, with training, anyone can develop and improve some ethnographic skills.

Based on our own research experiences, however, we would like to note several circumstances in which the lack of advanced training makes conducting research much more difficult. In these circumstances, special attention must be paid to training and practice for data collectors and analysts. Otherwise, research activities can lose focus, get out of hand, degenerate into mere collections of anecdotes, and confirm only what observers already know or expect, rather than identifying new knowledge. The result is very limited, if any, useful outcomes.

Such circumstances include instances when researchers do not know enough about the local community to choose research partners who can make good ethnographers, or when they make incorrect assumptions about the supposed capabilities of those whom they do hire. This can happen when research partners are hired from among willing and enthusiastic community residents or practicing professionals who have little or no formal training in ethnographic research methods.

━●━●━●━ **EXAMPLE 8.1**

WHEN A RESEARCH PARTNER UNDERSTANDS NEITHER
ETHNOGRAPHIC DESIGN NOR THE RESEARCH PURPOSE

In her study of a Punjabi community in California, Margaret Gibson hired as her co-director a member of the Punjabi community who also had a doctorate in the social sciences. She felt that having such a partner would be a good way to build rapport with the community and ensure that community perspectives were included in the research results. Unfortunately, the co-director was trained in psychology, and his research perspectives were considerably different from Gibson's. Also, he was from a region of the Punjab that was different from that of the community where the people who were to be studied came from, and he was neither liked nor trusted by some of them.

In addition, he had allegiances to constituencies in the community that were committed to ensuring that the research supported particular courses of action— even if the data gathered actually contradicted such an approach. The differences between Gibson and her co-director were irreconcilable. They resulted in the production of two reports: One was submitted by Gibson herself; the co-director created his own "minority report" (Gibson, 1988; Gibson, personal communication, 1998).

A second circumstance occurs when research partners familiar with quantitative research methods interpret ethnographic data to be "merely descriptive" or "anecdotal" and either are reluctant to pay attention to rigor when collecting such information or simply do not recognize it as data.

EXAMPLE 8.2

WHEN QUANTITATIVELY TRAINED FIELD-WORKERS DO NOT SEE
THE IMPORTANCE OF COLLECTING ETHNOGRAPHIC DATA

Staff of the Institute for Community Research (ICR) were asked by a national consulting firm to conduct a door-to-door survey of service satisfaction among Medicaid clients who had made the shift from state Medicaid funding to private Medicaid managed care services. The door-to-door survey was to be conducted only with those clients without telephones. The results were to be matched with those obtained from telephone surveying with the same instrument among those clients who had telephones. ICR staff noted that the survey questions were superficial and, because of the way they were asked, would not obtain valid data regarding clients' "real" views of the new service delivery arrangements. The consulting firm agreed to allow staff of the project to add a qualitative component to the instrument to see if they could collect better data on service delivery quality and accessibility. Interviewers were trained by ICR staff to conduct the survey, complete it, and then return to certain questions and probe more deeply into the responses. All field interviewers who remained with the project were able to conduct the quantitative interviews without a problem. Eleven of the 12 field interviewers did not conduct systematic qualitative interviews well, despite prior practice. When asked why, they claimed that the questions had already been answered quantitatively, and there was no point in asking them again.

Because of situations such as that in Example 8.2, we believe that except under special circumstances such as when trained ethnographers do both qualitative *and* quantitative data collection, ethnographic interviews should not be done by the same team members who collect survey data (and vice versa) because each will transpose their specialized set of interviewing skills into the others', muddying the methodological waters.

Finally, it is difficult—although not impossible—for service providers who see themselves as holding positions of authority over "clients," or who are primarily interested in obtaining information related to the services or other resources they can provide, to become the open-eyed learners called for by ethnographic research.

Ethnography requires ethnographers to build good working and personal relationships with and among groups of people with diverse and often conflicting opinions, lifestyles, and sociopolitical situations, while at the same time managing inevitable inter- and intragroup conflict sufficiently to produce good research results. This places special demands on the social, personal, and professional skills that researchers must bring to the field site with them.

If researchers can answer the following questions affirmatively, then ethnography definitely is an approach to research that they will find congenial.

- Do I feel at least relatively comfortable in new situations where the rules for behaving are not clear?
- Am I someone who is always interested in learning new things?
- Can I live without many of the comforts and conveniences (relatively speaking) of home?
- Do I find it relatively easy to build new relationships?
- Do I mind asking questions if I do not understand how things work or what is going on?
- Can I work for extended periods of time in situations that are ambiguous and unstructured?
- Can I begin projects without having to know exactly what I am going to do and in which direction the project is headed?

IDENTIFYING GOOD FIELD-WORKERS

Even the most experienced ethnographers find it difficult to carry out a study without assistance, especially in large, complex, or multisite projects. As a consequence, ethnographers build teams of assistants to facilitate the work. Building an ethnographic research team requires seeking out and hiring field researchers. As we have pointed out, however, finding good field researchers is not always easy. What makes a good field-worker, and how do we know one when we see one? In large part, the attributes that characterize good field-workers are the same attributes that characterize good ethnographers.

We believe that good field-workers are adventurous, resourceful, self-motivated, trustworthy, and able to take risks. They are people who are curious about what people believe and why people behave as they do, and they are willing and able to explore and document or describe in detail such cultural behavior and beliefs in the natural settings in which they occur, using the tools of ethnographic research. Someone who knows—or purports to know—everything there is to know about a community does not make a good field-worker because he or she will not uncover any new information about the community in question.

Sociability is an important element in fieldwork success. A good field-worker generally is a sociable person who enjoys talking with others and does not mind asking many personal questions. Observational skills are also helpful in fieldwork; people who are able to discover information through interpersonal interaction must be able to stand back and observe what goes on without being tempted to join the interaction.

Good field researchers must understand the arena of culture to be investigated and all of the possible additional contextual factors that could potentially relate to it or influence it. They also must have the skills and enthusiasm to seek out salient cultural behavior and to recognize it when it appears. Therefore, field researchers should be able to conceptualize and understand conceptual frameworks and models as they are developed in a team effort.

Finally, a good field-worker must be able to translate what he or she sees into text—either spoken or written. It matters less that a field-worker can *write* detailed text. It matters more that the field-worker can retain, recall, and record detail objectively, without confusing his or her own value judgments with strict observation. Example 8.3 displays some common kinds of inferences or value judgments that are taken to be field description of observations.

EXAMPLE 8.3

CONFUSING INFERENCE WITH DESCRIPTION

A field-worker noted in her observations that the respondents lived in an "old run down house in a bad neighborhood." She added that her particular respondent was "shy." Under probing by the project director to describe more completely what she *really* saw, the field-worker added that the house was built in a style common in the 1920s; most of the paint was peeling off; the roof had patches on it, and the screens on the windows and doors were torn. Most of the houses in the neighborhood were in the same condition; residents had told her that several were used by drug dealers, and that shootings were common on the street corners. These descriptors corroborated the field-worker's *inference* about the condition of the house and neighborhood, and they also permitted the project director and other readers to come to the same conclusion that the field-worker had made. Determining if the respondent really was "shy," however, was more difficult. The field-worker reported that the respondent had been reluctant to answer many questions, looked at the floor instead of meeting the field-worker's gaze, and spoke in a very quiet voice. The project director noted that the respondent was an American Indian, and that many of the questions in the field-worker's interview were quite sensitive for this population. Furthermore, the behavior that the field-worker described was common—and considered to be polite among American Indians. It probably was not an indicator of shyness but of cultural differences in interaction styles.

TABLE 8.1 Qualities of a Good Ethnographer

Characteristics	Skills
Adventurous	Observant
Resourceful	Communicative
Enthusiastic	Thinks conceptually
Self-motivated	Cognizant of cultural issues and behavior
Trustworthy	Reportorial
Risk-taking	Remembers well
Curious	Separates strict observation from personal bias or opinion
Sociable	Works well with a team

In summary, then, ethnographic field-workers should possess the characteristics and skills that are outlined in Table 8.1.

Ethnographers may hire students, other ethnographers, professionals, and community residents to be field researchers in a team study. It is wise to remember that there is no such thing as the perfect field-worker. Students or trained researchers from the community under study will have an insider's knowledge of the community, but their information will be limited to what is available to someone with their particular position in the community. As a consequence, they will have to find ways to extend their access to information and build their knowledge. Although students may have some training and experience developing conceptual frameworks, they will still need supervision, support, and guidance; after all, they are in the process of learning to be researchers. When students or other professionals are not from the research community, they also will need help gaining entrance to the community and adapting to it. Students, especially, will need assistance in gathering the required information.

Unlike nonresidents, community residents and students from the community may be very knowledgeable about some aspects of their community. However, they often need training in observational and interviewing techniques. If they can participate in the early development of the conceptual framework, they will be more able to hone their qualitative research skills, because they will be sensitive to the concepts underpinning the study and the kinds of data needed to answer research questions.

Professional people, regardless of their research experience, often have higher status and less time than do other people hired as assistants; these characteristics limit their access to both information and particular groups. Nevertheless, when ethnographic studies require part-time staff, community professionals such as teachers can be important additions to the research team, because they have the background necessary to understand both the research question and the importance of the research to the community. They also have many of the recording skills needed to do the work.

COLLECTING DATA
WITH A RESEARCH TEAM

The field-worker has a double responsibility—collecting ethnographic information about the topic in question in a team setting, and negotiating the environment in which the data are to be collected. Although some individuals are very good at both, most are likely to have a preference for one over the other. Also, they may have preferences for collecting one form of data over another. A talk with potential ethnographic field-workers will tell you whether they are willing and able to negotiate their own field situations, how much training and supervision they will need, and what kinds of data they are likely to be best at collecting.

EXAMPLE 8.4

MATCHING DATA COLLECTION STRATEGIES
WITH FIELD-WORKER PREFERENCES: I

A group of youth was collecting pilesort data on sexual behaviors of their peers. They were discussing different ways of collecting data on ethnic identity among high school students in the area. They listed surveys, pilesorts, individual interviews, group interviews, and observations. When asked individually which approach each would prefer, one young woman said she wanted to do one-on-one, in-depth interviews; a second, very outgoing young woman was interested in learning how to do focus groups; and a third, a rather shy young man, preferred the structure and social distance of the survey.

EXAMPLE 8.5

MATCHING DATA COLLECTION STRATEGIES
WITH FIELD-WORKER PREFERENCES: II

An interdisciplinary research team consisting of an anthropologist, an epidemiologist with a survey research background, and an anthropology student designed a study to collect information about children's activities and energy output, and mothers' perceptions of the relative value of the activities listed. In planning the study, one member of the team wanted to collect observational data about activities with which children were involved in the community, at school, and in and around homes. The second wanted to develop a survey instrument before conducting any observations; and the third wanted to record mothers' and children's histories of activity using in-depth interviews. To accommodate everyone's preferences while obtaining complementary data, the team was able to collect and use data using all three approaches.

EXAMPLE 8.6

MAKING COMPATIBILITY WITH THE REQUIRED DATA
COLLECTION STRATEGY A JOB QUALIFICATION

An independent research center sought an ethnographic researcher to head a team and to conduct field research among injection drug users in a local community. The project was one of a number of similar studies being carried out by a research consortium. Many staff members within the consortium agencies were very knowledgeable about the community in question and were available to introduce new members of the research team to the research setting. Two female candidates were interviewed. The first, when told that she would be expected to conduct observations and interviews, said that despite her communications background and her dissertation on a research topic similar to that outlined in the job description, she did not know how to enter the field and did not feel comfortable with the methodology. A second, who had no experience with the subject of the research but felt comfortable with the methodology, and who described how she would use resources at hand to enter the field, got the job.

◆•◆•◆

Identifying and Assembling a Research Team

Leadership is critical to a well-functioning ethnographic research team. Conceptual guidance, good working knowledge of personnel and budget management, and group team-building and facilitation skills are important qualities of an ethnographic team leader or principal investigator. Good team leaders recognize the value of team members and can identify ways in which they can offer team members individualized support in the areas of conceptualization, data collection, and analysis.

A well-functioning research team consists of individuals who have the skills to conduct research or other tasks and responsibilities to which they are assigned, and who know how to ask for help when they need it. Team members are willing to work with others to build common conceptual understandings, shared data coding and management systems, and partnerships in both the conduct of the research and the process of writing up the results.

Conflicts will invariably arise in the field, either among team members or between team members and community residents or institutional staff in settings where the research is being conducted. Effective team leaders will identify the potential for conflict before it becomes full blown and make good-faith efforts to resolve it by helping team members find common ground.

EXAMPLE 8.7

RESOLVING INTRATEAM CONFLICTS OVER HOW TO CARRY OUT A SURVEY

Team members in the ICR study of children's activities had a difference of opinion with respect to how the survey component of the study should be conducted in the field. One of the team members drew upon his expertise in epidemiological survey research to insist that the survey questions be asked in precisely the same way in every household setting, and with every mother-child team. The second, a member of the same ethnic group as that with whom the study was being conducted, argued that each setting and person was slightly different, and that some mothers were less educated or literate than others and could not understand the questions as they were stated. From his point of view, valid research could be conducted only if the questions were rephrased slightly to ensure understanding. The discontented epidemiologist called in Jean Schensul, the principal investigator, to "fix" the problem. The result was a compromise in which the ethnographer was free to modify the questions as necessary as long as the rephrasing of the questions was written into the survey and checked by the epidemiologist to ensure equivalence of meaning.

Committed team members should certainly communicate with the team leader when a conflict arises in the field setting, and they should seek help and expertise in resolving

it before it interrupts the research process. To be effective, team leaders should carefully investigate the situation before blaming team members for making a mistake, assume that team members did their best in the situation, and include them in attempts to resolve the problem.

Perhaps the most challenging issue faced by ethnographic investigators leading field research teams is the development of a common coding scheme and sharing of ethnographic data. This issue, dealt with more thoroughly in Book 5, Chapter 1, and Book 6, Chapter 2, calls for open dialogue. Dialogue should focus on the following:

- Clear understanding of the project among all team members
- Joint formulation of a coding scheme with primary and secondary coding categories
- Testing the coding categories by applying them to already collected text data

Cross Reference: See Book 5, Chapter 1, and Book 6, Chapter 2, for more information on constructing coding systems and using them in research teams

Team members who have not constructed or used coding taxonomies, who are accustomed to operationalized concepts "after the fact," or who have never operationalized their coding categories for the use of others may be reluctant to engage in these activities. A good team leader will convince such individuals that these activities are critically important to the collection of good data.

A more challenging issue is to convince ethnographic researchers who have never worked as part of a team that the data they collect themselves (and that they are accustomed to calling "their data") really belong to the research team. Some novice ethnographers have great difficulty writing up their fieldnotes so that they can be used by others, or sharing "their" data. Team leaders can find ways of permitting field researchers to maintain separately their personal thoughts and comments about their fieldnotes, while at the same time sharing their raw text data with other members of the team.

In team ethnography, where every team member theoretically "owns" or can access all the data, team members must find ways of collaborating on publications and dissemination activities. Team leaders should work with the team to create ground rules for developing publications and to establish the culture of the project in such a manner that ideas are shared and papers or other publications are authored jointly. These decisions or ground rules should be made clear to everybody on the team before a project begins. When communities or other partners become members of the research and writing "team," as is the case in participatory ethnographic research projects, they also should become co-authors on published papers. Roles that differentiate and use the respective skills of research team members should be developed to permit inclusion of team members who may be able to carry out only some of the technical research tasks, but without whose input the project would be impossible (Schensul, 1999).

Definition: Stakeholders are people or groups that are involved with the project or program and have a vested interest in its outcome

Definition: Gatekeepers are people who control access to information or to the research site itself

BUILDING RESEARCH PARTNERSHIPS

Ethnographic research teams are one sort of partnership—that is, a partnership of researchers with common research interests. Research teams may also consist of members other than researchers. Usually, they are **stakeholders** who are interested in using the data to improve their programs or the policies that affect their communities. Often, partners are **gatekeepers**. Sometimes, if the ethnographic research is part of a larger project that includes an intervention, stakeholders may include program, intervention, or outcomes evaluation staff.

There are several ways to organize research partnerships. One way is to build a very large project from the same organization base that includes representatives from every

interested constituency. This is an efficient structure because it centralizes decision making.

EXAMPLE 8.8

ORGANIZING A RESEARCH PARTNERSHIP FOR
REPRESENTATIVENESS AND CENTRALIZED DECISION MAKING

"Urban Women Against Substance Abuse" is a 5-year intervention study based at the Institute for Community Research with the purpose of preventing drug use and sex risk behavior in preadolescent and young adolescent girls. The program includes ethnographic researchers doing formative and curriculum-based ethnography on risk and resiliency behaviors and norms; an intervention staff that works closely with the ethnographers and conducts weekly group sessions with girls and their mothers; and an evaluation staff that conducts both qualitative and quantitative process and outcome evaluation. Partners (school principals, instructors, and agency heads) are members of informal advisory committees that provide support to the program at the Institute.

Not all funders or community partners support this kind of structure, however. Funders may not like it because they believe the placement of an outcome evaluation team in the same organization as the intervention will bias the results in favor of success. Participating or supporting agencies might not agree to it because it consolidates program resources—and, potentially, decision making—in the hands of a single organization.

A research consortium offers another alternative to partnership. In a research consortium, the participating agencies each have a specific role and contribution to make to the overall project. One agency may conduct the intervention, a second may conduct research on the formative process of implementing the intervention, and a third may be

Cross Reference: See Book 6, Chapter 2, for more information on building research teams and consortia

responsible for research on the intervention's outcomes. Or, if the research topic calls for a multiethnic research team, researchers from each ethnic/cultural group may be situated in organizations based in that ethnic community. Studies organized in this way require both a policy team and a management team. The policy team consists of the leaders of the organizations—senior people responsible for the study. They usually include the principal investigators and agency heads or senior administrators who can make major directional decisions about the study. The management team includes the day-to-day field researchers and managers of the study (and usually the lead researchers or principal investigators). Consortium structures can be challenging. Some typical problems are the following:

- Decisions at the policy level may not be translated effectively to the management level.
- Researchers on the management team report to supervisors in their home organizations *and* research supervisors who may be based in other participating organizations, leaving room for confusion in direction and gaps in performance.
- Decisions to hire may be made jointly, but termination lies in the hands of immediate supervisors. The project director may not be able to address directly poor performance on the part of a project staff member based in another organization.
- Participating organizations have different personnel policies, salary levels, benefits, and organizational cultures and expectations, all of which have implications for project team cohesion.

The following example shows how consortia, if well planned, can offer projects the advantages of better and more rigorous research design opportunities and the informational and staffing resources of a wide variety of organizations.

EXAMPLE 8.9

ADVANTAGES OF A WELL-PLANNED CONSORTIUM

For the past 10 years, the Institute for Community Research (ICR) has been an initiator and/or full participant in both AIDS research and research and intervention studies in Hartford, Connecticut. The first citywide AIDS study was conducted by a consortium consisting of three organizations—the Institute, the Hispanic Health Council, and the Urban League of Greater Hartford—and the local health department. These organizations had been working together to convey the message that HIV infection was a problem affecting the entire city, and not just a single ethnic or otherwise designated community. The benefits of a consortium study were its ability to convey the citywide importance of the problem; the participation of organizations representing the major ethnic groups in the city; and the involvement of the local health department, which could disseminate the data immediately.

The project was a two-phase study of AIDS knowledge, attitudes, and behaviors in adults between the age of 18 and 49. Phase 1 took place in a multiethnic "bellwether" neighborhood; Phase 2 took place in two areas of the city and four neighborhoods where most African American and Puerto Rican residents lived and where two large public housing projects, the sites of known drug use, were located.

During the planning phase, before submission of the grant, each organization defined its contribution and role in relation to the project. When the grant was awarded to the grantee organization, representatives from each participating agency formed a steering committee that met weekly to plan and review the progress of the project. The steering committee allocated responsibilities equally across the participating organizations. The project coordinator, based at the ICR, reported to the director of the ICR on a daily basis and to the steering committee for project monitoring. She managed the data collection team and coordinated the collection of more than 600 interviews. Data were entered and analyzed at the Hispanic Health Council and presented to the steering committee for interpretation. The Urban League was responsible for ethnographic data collection in housing projects and two target neighborhoods. The final report was written by representatives from all participating organizations and submitted to the funder as a team effort. The published reports are cited as a product of the consortium: the AIDS Community Research

Group. This group then evolved into the Consortium Advocating for AIDS Prevention (the CAAP Consortium), a group of 7 to 10 agencies (depending on the project) conducting research, intervention, drug treatment, testing and counseling, needle exchange, and evaluation and dissemination of research results. This group has continued its work for almost a decade.

Well-functioning consortia produce very high-quality data and better interpretation of research results. They also provide the infrastructure for better and broader use of the study for program or community improvement purposes. Perhaps the most important thing to keep in mind when planning a research consortium is to discuss these and other

 Key point   issues during the planning phase of the project. *The best functioning consortia take nothing for granted and spell out working arrangements in written documents, including procedures for interorganizational conflict resolution, well before the project begins.*

Studies conducted by individuals, as well as those carried out in research teams or partnerships, raise numerous ethical issues. Some of these issues stem from conditions in the field, whereas others are implicit in the nature of the research topic. Still others have to do with the race, religion, culture, age, gender, and health status of participants, as well as with culturally sensitive or potentially illegal or legally reportable behaviors in which they might be engaged. Ethical issues are of special interest in ethnography, because researchers engaged in face-to-face observations and interviews in the field can and do stumble upon activities that may be unethical—from their point of view or that of the community—illegal, or even, in some cases, dangerous to the lives of participants or others in the community. Furthermore, they develop intimate relationships with respondents that may require or invite them to engage in activities that they would not otherwise consider. In the final chapter of this book, we review some ethical considerations and dilemmas in the conduct of ethnographic research and the institutional and other structures available to help resolve them.

Cross Reference: We address these ethical issues further in Book 6

NOTE

1. See LeCompte and Preissle (1993), Chapter 5, for an extensive discussion of the differences between everyday thinking and thinking-like-a-researcher.

9 ❂─❂─❂

ETHICAL TREATMENT OF RESEARCH PARTICIPANTS AND CARE FOR HUMAN RELATIONSHIPS

❂ All researchers are bound by codes of ethics to protect the people whom they study against treatment that would be harmful to them—physically, financially, emotionally, or in terms of their reputation.[1] This does not mean that researchers can do only research that involves no risk at all to study participants. It does mean that if risks do exist, the benefits of the study should outweigh the risks, and—and this is far more important—the people incurring the risks should fully understand what the short- and long-term risks are and volunteer to incur them. These issues are usually referred to and addressed under the heading "protection from risk to human subjects".

The general areas of concern with respect to the protection of research participants involve the following:

- Whether or not the people who are being studied have consented to be a part of the study.
- Whether they understand what will happen to them and the risks involved as a consequence of the study sufficiently well to be able to give informed consent.

183

■ Whether, having consented to participate in a study, their rights to privacy, confidentiality, or anonymity will be respected.

THE HISTORY OF CONCERN FOR THE ETHICAL TREATMENT OF RESEARCH PARTICIPANTS

In the United States, protection of human research subjects has received increasing attention from governmental agencies and the community of scholars. Revelations about two specific sets of studies done in the mid-20th century were particularly dramatic in pointing the way to better protection for all classes of study participants. The first, the "Tuskegee Studies," involved African American male prisoners infected with syphilis. Although effective treatment for syphilis was available, experimenters interested in tracking the progression of the disease to the point of death gave one group of men a placebo rather than the antibiotics that would have cured them. They did not inform the men that they were not likely to be cured, nor that an effective cure was readily available. These men, already limited in their ability to make choices, did not have the opportunity to understand or agree to participate in the study. The rationale of the researchers was that the men otherwise received good custodial care, and that medical technology would be enhanced by the increased knowledge that studies of the men's ultimate deaths from syphilis made possible. However, both clinical and historical data already existed that provided much of the information that the study ostensibly would generate.

The second group of studies, the "Milgram Experiments" (Milgram, 1963), were done by a social psychologist, Stanley Milgram, who was curious as to why many German people during World War II violated their own stated principles by participating in the extermination of Jews. Milgram set up experiments in which research subjects were led to believe that they were administering increasingly painful electric shocks to punish individuals who were not working quickly enough on tasks assigned to them in the experiment. The individuals "receiving" shocks actually were Milgram's partners in the study and only acted as if they were in pain. However, the research subjects were encouraged by the researcher—a scientifically authoritative figure whose status simulated the authority of the Nazi government—to continue to administer shocks even at levels they were led to believe could be lethal. Although the research subjects were told the true story of the experiment after it was over, were introduced to the people whom they had supposedly shocked, and could see that they were unharmed, the shame and guilt engendered by participating in the experiment haunted them for years.

In the first case, research subjects not only were not told that the treatment they received while participating would not cure them, but they were also deprived of known treatment that *would* have cured them. In the second case, research subjects were not made cognizant of the long-term emotional damage they might suffer. More recently, reports have surfaced of experiments done during the 1950s to 1970s on the effects of radiation on children, pregnant women, and people with illnesses. These people were given radiation without their knowledge and/or consent. Other studies during the same period used radioactive agents to track the uptake of nutritional elements in the same populations. Both sets of studies were unethical because subjects neither knew about nor consented to be in the studies; in many cases, the subjects were legally incapable of giving consent because they were children in custodial institutions.

In 1997, another incident occurred—described in Example 9.1—that confirmed that our concern about ethical treatment of human subjects is not based simply on historical examples. As we noted earlier, researchers in the United

States cannot use traditional no-treatment control groups —that is, comparison groups in which no intervention is offered—in cases where some form of treatment exists and lack of treatment would constitute a grave risk to members of the control group.

EXAMPLE 9.1　　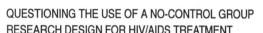

QUESTIONING THE USE OF A NO-CONTROL GROUP
RESEARCH DESIGN FOR HIV/AIDS TREATMENT

In 1997, a group of researchers initiated a study of ways to slow the spread of HIV/AIDS among women of childbearing age and their children. They reasoned that good health and nutrition, information about prevention and transmission of HIV/AIDS, and adequate pre- and postnatal care might well help many at-risk or already HIV-infected women survive longer, and also might help their babies remain uninfected. They also wanted to determine if less-than-heroic treatment with existing anti-AIDS drugs would be helpful in cases where the kind of multiple drug treatment currently used by more affluent AIDS patients in the United States was prohibitively expensive. Thus, their design called for a study much like the Tuskegee Syphilis Study: They would set up a number of treatment groups and one control group. All groups would receive information about health, nutrition, and HIV/AIDS prevention, as well as pre- and postnatal care. The treatment groups would receive varying types and amounts of drugs—particularly AZT—known to be effective against HIV/AIDS. Of particular interest was the role of varying amounts of AZT in limiting the transmission of AIDS from mothers to their newborn children—if it were administered during the woman's pregnancy. The control group would receive a placebo, but no real drug treatment.

U.S. government regulations prohibit such a study from being carried out in the United States, so researchers organized their study in Africa, where HIV/AIDS has become epidemic and where the costly AZT treatment available in the United States cannot be provided widely. They recruited subjects by asking women who had just been tested for both pregnancy and HIV infection if they wanted to participate in a study that "could help their baby remain healthy." Most of the women who consented to participate indicated later on that they were too confused and frightened at their diagnoses—and at finding out simultaneously that they were to become mothers—to understand clearly what the study was about. Most—even those in the control

group—believed that they were receiving real drug therapy. The researchers argued that even the women in the control group benefitted from participating in the program, because they were receiving better prenatal care. They were, however, heavily criticized on two accounts: for implementing in a poor, nonwhite country a study that they could not have done in their own country, and for not obtaining truly "informed" consent from the participants (Levine, 1998; Lurie & Wolfe, 1997).

Studies such as the Tuskegee and Milgram experiments led to constraints on medical, social science, and natural science research on human beings. The example above demonstrates that continued vigilance must be exercised, especially with respect to populations that are vulnerable because they are under stress, feel coerced, are ill or illiterate, or are less knowledgeable about research. This principle holds for any population, regardless of location in the United States or elsewhere in the world. It also makes clear that researchers cannot circumvent the standards existing in their own institution or country by doing research in another site. Researchers are legally required to conform to the standards applicable within their own institution or country, regardless of where the research is carried out.

Professional Codes of Ethics

Proper treatment of human research subjects by U.S. researchers is regulated in several ways. First, professional associations such as the American Psychological Association, the American Medical Association, the Society for Applied Anthropology, and the American Anthropological Association all have codes of ethics that spell out the standards of care to which members of its discipline are held with regard to the people they study. These codes, however, are general and informational rather than mandates requiring behavior. Most professional research organizations also have ethics committees that review ethical issues as they arise in the course of research, as well as publications that portray ethical dilemmas and ways in which they are resolved in the field. These tools for considering ethical decisions are especially important where ethnography is being conducted, because ethical issues that were not anticipated prior to the start of the research often arise in the course of face-to-face interviews and field-based research once the study begins. Stricter controls than those possible under guidance by codes of professional ethics are exercised by the U.S. federal government through policies established by the Office of Protection from Research Risks, an administrative branch of the Department of Health and Human Services, and by **Institutional Review Boards,** which are established by federal administrative regulations.

Definition: An Institutional Review Board is a committee set up by an organization to review, approve, and regulate research conducted by its members, on its premises, or under its sponsorship

INSTITUTIONAL REVIEW BOARDS

All universities, public schools, hospitals and medical centers, and nonprofit organizations conducting research or evaluation studies have Institutional Review Boards (IRBs) that review any proposal involving human clients, constituencies, participants, subjects, or members. IRBs are established under a mandate by the U.S. government and have the authority to approve or reject, call for changes in, suspend, or terminate research that is deemed harmful to participants, careless, or unethical. They also can oversee research projects and withdraw their approval, stopping a study if the researcher deviates from approved practice in ways that are harmful to subjects or if the study has unintended and deleterious impacts on its participants.

IRB approval is required for all research funded by the U.S. government and for virtually all research carried out by university researchers, because their institutions receive support from the federal government. It is also required for researchers working in or with any institution in the United States that receives, either directly or indirectly, funds from the U.S. government. In most cases, researchers must seek approval from the relevant IRBs before they can begin their studies. Particular guidelines are spelled out with respect to certain protected classes of people, which include *all* children under the age of 18; anyone with a mental health or cognitive disability or with a physical disability that requires a legal guardian; people who are ill or women who are pregnant if their physical condition is related to the topic of the study; people who are in treatment centers, prisons, or other custodial institutions; and individuals whose known participation in a study might subject them to civil or criminal prosecution—such as users of illegal drugs.

Obtaining approval or **certification** from an IRB requires submitting a detailed proposal to an IRB for any study. Components of a proposal for IRB approval include the following:

Definition: Certification of a research study means that it has been approved by an IRB

- A description of the study and its purpose
- A description of the population to be studied and how its members will be selected for the study
- A description of the interventions that researchers plan to implement, if any
- Enumeration and description of the data collection methods to be used
- Information about how proposed subjects will be informed about the study and what will happen to them if they agree to participate
- An assessment of the risks and benefits of the studies to participants and to the general population
- A description of how the researcher intends to protect the identity of participants
- A statement assuring participants of their right to participate or withdraw at any point without consequence to themselves or their families

■ The addresses and phone numbers of the researchers and of the responsible people in the researchers' institutions

All of the above-listed components must be described with sufficient clarity that research subjects can reasonably consent—or withhold their consent—to participation. In most cases, researchers will be required to obtain written consent to participate from the potential participants, as well as from the participants' legal guardians, if the participants are children or are incapacitated. Under most circumstances, simplified written assent also must be obtained from children who are research participants.

Researchers also must provide to both the IRB and participants a description of the strategies they will use to protect the privacy of participants. In general, researchers are asked to guarantee confidentiality or anonymity. Anonymity is fully possible only when the researchers themselves cannot connect a specific individual to the data collected from that individual—as in the case of questionnaires that are mailed out and returned unsigned by the respondent and uncoded by the researcher. In survey research, where interviewers actually interview respondents in face-to-face encounters, confidentiality is usually ensured by removing names and other identifiers from the database and analyzing the data in aggregate form.

However, ethnographers often cannot use all of these procedures. Much of the time, ethnographic researchers know who their informants are, see them repeatedly, and are seen by others in the community while conducting interviews and observing with community members. In addition, ethnographic fieldnotes may contain descriptions of individuals or situations that, when read by other members of the research team, can reveal the identities of respondents. For these reasons, ethnographers cannot assure participants of anonymity at all times. They can, however, make every effort to keep confidential the identity of specific individuals. This can be done by using pseudonyms, altering certain biographical data, and even disguising the site or time period in which data are collected. We caution researchers to use these strategies even when, as may be the case, participants would like to have their true identity revealed, because it is never possible to assess adequately in advance which data, if revealed, might become harmful to an informant. Furthermore, ethnographers can and should use guidelines for interviewing that preclude citing information obtained from other members of the research community, or otherwise revealing their knowledge of situations that could have come only from known sources. Finally, ethnographers may not be able to protect respondents from complete anonymity within the research team. However, especially if text data are to be shared, procedures should be in place to make sure that fieldnotes do not reveal participants' real identities, addresses, or other information that could allow them to be identified.

IRBs usually require that researchers provide assurance from the research site that the research project has been approved. For example, LeCompte had to supply letters supporting her research from the principals of each of the schools she studied, as well from as from the superintendent of the school districts involved before the university IRB would approve her study. She also had to obtain approval from the IRBs of the individual districts. If the research is to be conducted in community settings, where gatekeepers such as principals cannot be found, letters of support from community-based organizations that serve the communities can be sought. Alternatively, these organizations can be brought into the study as partners to ensure as much as possible that protection of community interests lies in the hands of others besides the researcher.

Before federally funded research grants are approved (and in some cases, such as the National Institute of Mental Health, before proposals are even reviewed), a researcher must seek approval from the IRB of the site in which the research is to be conducted, in addition to his or her own supervising institution's IRB. Many school districts, funding agencies, health care agencies, and social service agencies also have IRBs or their equivalents. To illustrate, in a federally funded study of high-risk drug use among adolescents that was just beginning in Hartford, Connecticut, Schensul obtained **assurances**, which are required by the federal Office of Protection from Research Risk, from three subcontracting institutions guaranteeing that they agreed to perform in accordance with Institute for Community Research IRB requirements. For this study, even though the only responsibility that one of the subcontractors had was to help Hartford researchers analyze data, the mere possibility that he might come into contact with the data required a special assurance.

In Book 6, *Researcher Roles and Research Partnerships*, we detail the general procedures that researchers must follow to gain IRB approval. Here, we simply urge researchers to be aware of the need to obtain such approvals, and to secure the guidelines for doing so from both the funders and the individual institutions involved. Failure to obtain approval and to follow the rules for ethical treatment of human subjects can cause an IRB to stop a research project in its tracks. It can also prevent federal or other funders from initiating funding on a grant that has been approved until a review has taken place and the required forms are obtained.

Definition: Assurances are documents produced by IRBs to describe their procedures for ensuring that researchers in their institution will conform to regulations concerning protection of human subjects from research risk

Cross Reference: See Book 6, Chapter 1, for more information on how to obtain IRB approval

SPECIAL CONCERNS AND ETHICAL
RESPONSIBILITIES OF ETHNOGRAPHERS

Institutional protections are very important in ensuring protection of participants and even communities in a study. It is even more crucial that researchers understand and abide by ethical considerations underpinning these protections when doing their work. This is especially important for ethnographers. Ethnographers are not usually involved in risky clinical experiments, although if they and other members of the study team are conducting formative or evaluation research in such studies, they should be alert to possible human subjects issues. Unique to ethnography, however, is the practice of interacting with people for long periods of time, which gives ethnographers considerably greater opportunity to learn secrets and intimate details of people's lives. This is precisely the kind of information that could cause people harm in their communities if it were disclosed. The long-term presence of ethnographers in the field may also be confusing to study participants because the boundaries between friendship and professional research conduct become blurred. In such situations, ethical conduct in research interacts with ethical conduct in the context of personal relationships. Ethnographers may observe or hear about illegal, dangerous, or potentially abusive activities in the course of fieldwork. In some cases, their observations may invoke the legal requirement to report the incident or behavior to authorities.

We believe that honesty and openness in relationships with research partners and participants leads to better ethnography; honest and open relationships make people willing to give researchers access to better, more valid, and more copious data.

Furthermore, the long-term involvement of ethnographers with their subjects makes it as difficult for ethnographers to hide secrets as it is for subjects! Attempts to engage in covert research or subterfuge of any kind are made more difficult in field ethnography. Playing a role day in and day out is difficult, and because ethnographers are not really trained to be duplicitous, the chances of being unmasked are greater. Nevertheless, given the blurring of the lines between research and personal relationships mentioned above, study participants can forget that the ethnographer is there to do research. Researchers should feel obliged to explain the study repeatedly, especially when entering a new situation where those present may not be aware that research is being conducted in their setting or community.

EXAMPLE 9.2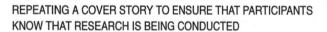

REPEATING A COVER STORY TO ENSURE THAT PARTICIPANTS
KNOW THAT RESEARCH IS BEING CONDUCTED

Even though LeCompte and her research assistants had been working with the Arts Focus program at Highline Middle School for more than 2 years, they still had to remind participants of the purpose of their study and identify themselves in every meeting and interview as those "researchers from the university who are studying the Arts Program." New teachers, as well as students and their parents who were new to the building, had not been present at the initial meetings when LeCompte and the research team were introduced; the students also tended to forget the identity of any adult in the school who was not their own immediate or former teacher.

Ethical considerations, then, come into play during the design phase of the research process as the researcher seeks relevant approvals and consent from individuals and institutions. They continue as researchers enter the field, establish relationships with people, and begin to collect data. We have already described how researchers become "special friends" with research participants; the specialness of these relationships has to do not only with the fact that such friendships were initiated for the purpose of gathering information (Spradley, 1979), but also with the fact that, unlike ordinary friendships, these should be governed by quite specific and codified standards of care for privacy and for protection from harm. Friendships formed during ethnographic research differ from other friendships in other ways as well. Because ethnographers need to hear from all voices in a setting and to learn about issues on all sides of problems, their friendships must span boundaries across groups that may be in conflict (cf. Gonzalez et al., 1982).

The reports that ethnographers write at the end of their studies, and even the feedback they give during the course of a study, often involve telling people things that they do not want to hear (LeCompte, 1994; McDade, 1987). Certain members of groups within the setting may view such disclosures as harmful to them. This is especially likely to occur when the setting is complex and when many constituencies participate, or have interests, in the results of the research. In these cases, researchers may be accused of "taking sides" if they disclose incompetence, inconsistencies, noncompliance, mal- or misfeasance, or just plain ignorance of issues—even if the foregoing are key to the solution of problems that the ethnographer was hired to explore and clarify.

Ethnographic field-workers also face problems of reciprocity. Providing information to researchers is not a one-way street; more and more, those who provide information want to receive something in return, even if that something involves no more than the goodwill and attention of the researcher. Quite often, however, reciprocity involves exchange of far more tangible goods, services, or information. Traditionally, ethnographers tried hard to build their reports primarily on "volunteered" information, on the grounds that information that was paid for in any way could be tainted by the self-interest of the informant. Although this degree of purism is now recognized as unnecessary and probably unfeasible, questions do arise about the degree to which the kind of exchange affects the kind of information proffered to researchers. For example, in some ethnographic studies, where key informants or local experts are interviewed for long periods of time, or repeatedly, they may be offered material compensation for their time. Survey respondents may also be paid for their time. Generally, however, the decision to pay respondents is based on whether or not they lose financial resources by agreeing to be interviewed (e.g., if they are paid or earn income on an hourly basis); and whether or not such reciprocity is possible, necessary, and scientifically appropriate. In ethnographic studies where a large sample of respondents is to be interviewed only once, and no more tangible reciprocity is possible, a modest payment or small gift is not uncommon.

EXAMPLE 9.3 ━●━●━●━

TOKEN REMUNERATION FOR PARTICIPATION IN AN ETHNOGRAPHY

The study of children's activity levels carried out by researchers at the Institute for Community Research required nightly involvement of parents and children in taking measurements of energy outputs. Mothers and children were given a small gift certificate and a gift (a baseball hat or hair ribbon) after the data were collected. Similarly, in a school-based intervention with a longitudinal outcome evaluation design—mother and daughter pairs were asked to return to fill out assessment instruments three times over 3 years—each pair received a small payment of $10.00 per visit or interview, and participated in a "party" celebration with food and entertainment.

━●━●━

In many applied or collaborative ethnographic projects, the researchers can provide research services or conduct studies for participants that participants would like to have done, but for which they have no time themselves.

EXAMPLE 9.4

EXCHANGING RESEARCH AND CONSULTING NOT RELATED
TO THE STUDY FOR PARTICIPANTS' INFORMATION

LeCompte routinely helped teachers and administrators in Pinnacle School District, in The Learning Circle Program, and at Arts Focus in Highline Middle School to design surveys and assessment instruments to collect data in which they were interested. She did library searches for busy teachers and conducted interviews with them to record their recollections of how programs were developing. The latter served two purposes: They constituted data for LeCompte's monitoring of the program, but they also created a journal for the teachers of their year's work—a journal that they did not have time to keep themselves. She also photographed program activities, giving copies of the photos to the schools. Again, the photos were part of LeCompte's database, but they also created a scrapbook for the school.

One of the most delicate issues in fieldwork is that of exploitation; in traditional ethnographic fieldwork, the local community studied benefited little from the fact that their lives had been studied and written about. By contrast, the researcher benefited greatly in terms of publications, research grants, and tenured positions in universities and research institutions. Applied or collaborative ethnographic research, such as we describe in this book, is criticized less on such grounds because it is not done except insofar as the researchers and the participants agree that a study would benefit the community or help it to solve its problems. Nevertheless, it is possible for researchers to be regarded as exploiters who use data about the people they study to make more money and attain higher prestige than the people in the communities being studied. To forestall this accusation, researchers can work with community or institutional partners to find public ways to make the data available and usable and to give participants credit for their assistance. Furthermore, ethnographic studies often lead to other opportunities for developing interventions or programs of service to the community. Ethnographers who are situated in stable institutions may be able to use their research and their community partnerships to create new research and development opportunities that enhance quality of life and meet a variety of needs in the research community.

In addition to the above considerations, which are relevant during the study, we also believe that ethical considerations extend beyond the actual study itself. Traditional ethnographers worried about saying goodbye to people in the field, and about the reciprocal nature of the relationships that developed between themselves and participants in the study based on friendship, good fellowship, jobs, material and emotional support, and attention. Contemporary ethnographers also have to be worried about the impact of their research results once they have left. In addition to the above-mentioned interdependencies, contemporary ethnographers have an ethical responsibility to come up with the best and most truthful interpretation of data possible; they can be aided in this process by inducing research partners to share in the interpretations. Sharing in interpretation, however, can be complicated when research partners cannot agree among themselves, or when they give interpretations that would violate assurances of confidentiality given in exchange for disclosure of critical information. Field relationships can be complicated further when research participants and partners expect commitments from researchers to help with ongoing solutions to problems identified in the research—despite the other professional and personal commitments researchers might have outside the confines of the study at hand. All of these issues must be handled with care, diplomacy, and respect for all. Certainly, it is best for the researcher to avoid misunderstandings by explaining beforehand what constraints to implementation might arise following the study, and to review these at the end to avoid disappointments.

Often, the ethnographer lives in the community where the study is being conducted. This poses additional problems and obligations, especially when funding for the study runs out but the ethnographer is still present and visible. In such cases, it is useful for the researcher to identify other resources to assist in utilization of the research results so that community partners do not feel disappointed or deserted when the ethnographer can no longer provide the services and resources once provided by his or her project. Although this is not always possible, the best and most exciting solution is to work with the community to continue the project by soliciting additional funds and/or designing intervention strategies in which the ethnographer can also participate. Sometimes, a decision must be made to engage in such work on a voluntary basis in order to maintain critical relationships with research partners.

EXAMPLE 9.5

CONTINUING TO COLLABORATE WHEN THE MONEY RUNS OUT

Researchers at the Institute for Community Research conducted a 2-year census survey in partnership with more than 80 community organizations, municipal planning councils, parent-teacher organizations, and schools. The study was intended to involve communities in understanding, interpreting, and critiquing the census; constructing an equivalent instrument; collecting data; learning how to analyze it; and using it for planning purposes. Researchers also partnered with neighborhoods and municipalities to identify issues unique to each location, using focus groups and key informant interviews. A neighborhood-based special issues section, which included closed- and open-ended questions, was added to each interview schedule. Five centralized organizations well known and respected in the region were invited to take a more active role in the study, and they participated in the enumeration of households, interviews, and debriefing and discussions around the data and results. These organizations also agreed to handle data files and other project data and to make these data available to their constituencies when the first phase of the project was over.

The first part of the study included activities up to the point of data analysis. Data were analyzed by ICR staff and reviewed by organizations in each neighborhood and municipality for accuracy; participants in the discussions contributed greatly to interpretation of the data. A booklet was produced that summarized data and provided a community-based history of each neighborhood. Neighborhoods were given copies of the booklets for distribution, and neighborhood organizations were offered copies of their neighborhood's data on disk.

The second phase of the project was to have trained staff of the five organizations central to the study in data analysis and use of the data files and histories. This phase of the project was not funded by local groups that had funded the first phase. These funders agreed to dissemination of the data through public presentations but did not see the utility of helping local organizations to use the data for community-based planning purposes. Neither was it possible, without additional funding, to analyze data gathered on special issues in each neighborhood. This decision placed the Institute in a precarious position with regard to some neighborhood organizations that claimed that they had collaborated with the project and were promised results that they did not receive. ICR staff volunteered many hours of additional work to live up to their original commitment to serve these organizations as promised in order to maintain their relationship as research partners with a commitment to community development.

➤•➤•➤

THE ETHICAL RESPONSIBILITIES OF ETHNOGRAPHERS IN THE ABSENCE OF AN IRB OR FORMAL INSTITUTIONAL CONSTRAINTS

Many ethnographers are self-employed or do freelance work as consultants, program developers, or evaluators outside of their regular employment. Still others work in nonprofit or for-profit organizations that do not have IRBs. Are such researchers still bound by the constraints customarily imposed by Institutional Review Boards? We believe that they are. The absence of formal watchdog organizations that establish, review, and enforce systematic procedures for ensuring the ethical treatment of human subjects does not give researchers permission to exercise lower standards of care for the people they study.

We advocate that all researchers include in their research designs and proposal documents the same approvals, assurances, and safeguards that they would have to provide to an IRB. We also recommend that they make these documents available to the study site and the research participants or their representatives. Even if the only reason for so doing is to guard against some future and unanticipated criticisms, such documents can provide insurance against embarrassment and even lawsuits. Furthermore, doing so ensures that researchers will not forget about their obligations to informants and other community members in the excitement of organizing a new project.

DISSEMINATION OF RESEARCH RESULTS

Dissemination of research results concerns responsibility to the various "communities" to which the ethnographic researcher owes allegiance. These communities include the people in the settings in which the research is conducted and those who are involved as participants, respondents, informants, and partners in the research; other professional colleagues; funders; institutions in which the researchers are based (e.g., universities, research institutes, and nonprofits); other institutions and policymakers; and the public at large. What results these audiences will need and how they will use them should be considered before and during the conduct of the research, as well as once the research is completed. The chapters in Book 7 cover three main ways in which ethnography can be disseminated and used:

Cross Reference: See Book 7 for different approaches to dissemination and use of ethnographic research

- Guiding policymakers
- Influencing the conduct and quality of service and educational programs
- Creating and fostering public programs

In this final section of Book 1, we outline some of the main considerations to keep in mind when using ethnographic data.

First, the audiences should be identified at the start of the project. Of course, it is never possible to know in advance all of the audiences that might be interested in a set of research results. But ethnographic researchers should be familiar with at least some of them and should, if possible, work with members of the target audience to gear both the selection of results to be reported and the style in which the results are reported to their specific needs and interests. A scientific audience will want to know more about research methods and approaches to data analysis. A policy-oriented audience will want to be convinced of the validity, reliability, and generalizability of the research results. Community audiences will want to know what the results mean for themselves and their communities.

Cross Reference: See Book 2 for discussion of reliability, validity, and generalizability in ethnographic research

See Books 5 and 7 for information on audiences

Ethnographic research usually produces large amounts of text data that are difficult to summarize succinctly. Researchers should be able to identify the major results of the research and present them in ways that are readily understood using graphic visual aids, "bulleted" overhead or slide projections, and illustrative vignettes and case materials. People who have access to sophisticated, reliable, and easy-to-use computerized graphics equipment can do particularly effective presentations; these should always be pretested and previewed for their level of understandability and their cultural appropriateness to the specific audience.

Researchers and respondents or community cultural experts may have differing interpretations of research results. Such differences will be important to resolve for purposes of influencing policymakers, because researchers and community partners can be more convincing if they present a united front. When the results of research have significant implications for institutions such as schools or hospitals, or for policies that affect the lives of community residents by changing the customary flow of information, services, or income, these implications should be discussed with representatives beforehand. Such discussions are not for the purpose of changing research results or withholding information. Instead, it is both ethical and considerate to permit institutions that have been involved in the research to prepare for the implications of information that could influence their welfare or well-being.

For public programming purposes, it may be more important to highlight differences as a means of educating the public. We recommend that this be done with the partnership and support of members of the collaborating community in order to avoid misrepresentation or dissent within the community itself.

Cross Reference: See the chapters by Hess and by Williamson, Brecher, Glasser, and Schensul in Book 7 for a discussion of how ethnographers can resolve such differences and turn community diversity into an asset

EXAMPLE 9.6

RESOLVING INTRACOMMUNITY CONFLICTS IN A PROGRAM ABOUT TAINO/PUERTO RICAN CULTURE

In a panel discussion accompanying a recent controversial exhibit on Taino history and culture at the Institute for Community Research, the speakers, all of whom were Puerto Rican, had different historical, cultural, and political perspectives on the status and continuity of Taino culture. The dialogue that ensued as a result of these differences was enlightening for both panelists and the audience and resulted in a re-inforcing of cultural history and identity within the framework of difference. However, such a discussion could have been divisive if the panel had been organized to present one—rather than multiple—perspectives on Taino history and identity.

Maintaining confidentiality is critically important when presenting ethnographic data to the public. Care should be taken to avoid citing specific locations and street addresses, or describing individual case materials in such a way that the individuals described could be identified. When the products of research are photographs, audiotapes, or videotapes, signed releases or other forms of agreement should be obtained before they are shown to the public. Other considerations with respect to dissemination and continued collaboration in research and practice with study sites will be reviewed in greater detail in Book 7.

CONCLUSION

We have now presented you, the reader, with an overview of the ethnographic research process, from its design and implementation through dissemination and utilization of research results. We hope that the preceding pages have both intrigued you and stimulated your desire to put ethnography to work in your own projects and institutions. Because this single volume is not intended to tell the complete story, we now urge you to continue exploring how to "do ethnography" in the other books of the **Ethnographer's Toolkit**:

- Book 2: *Essential Ethnographic Methods: Observations, Interviews, and Questionnaires*
- Book 3: *Enhanced Ethnographic Methods: Audiovisual Techniques, Focused Group Interviews, and Elicitation Techniques*
- Book 4: *Mapping Social Networks, Spatial Data, and Hidden Populations*
- Book 5: *Analyzing and Interpreting Ethnographic Data*
- Book 6: *Researcher Roles and Research Partnerships*
- Book 7: *Using Ethnographic Data: Interventions, Public Programming, and Public Policy*

We hope that your excursion into ethnography will be an adventure!

NOTE

1. For a review of the ways in which different philosophical approaches to ethics are applied to ethnographic and qualitative research, see Deyhle, Hess, and LeCompte (1992).

REFERENCES

Berger, P. L., & Luckmann, T. (1967). *The social construction of reality: A treatise in the sociology of knowledge.* Garden City, NY: Anchor.

Bernard, H. R. (1988). *Research methods in cultural anthropology.* Newbury Park, CA: Sage.

Bernard, H. R. (1995). *Research methods in anthropology: Qualitative and quantitative approaches* (2nd ed.). Walnut Creek, CA: AltaMira.

Bott, E. (1957). *Family and social networks: Roles, norms and external relationships in ordinary urban families.* London: Tavistock.

Bourgeois, P. (1996, September). *The moral economies of homeless heroin addicts: San Francisco shooting encampments.* Paper presented at the American Anthropological Association Commission on AIDS Research and Education Conference, Washington, DC.

Burnett, J. (1974). On the analogy between cultural acquisition and ethnographic method. *Anthropology and Education Quarterly, 5*(1), 25-29.

Campbell, D. T., & Stanley, J. C. (1963). Experimental and quasi-experimental designs for research on teaching. In N. L. Gage (Ed.), *The handbook of research on teaching* (pp. 171-247). Chicago: Rand McNally.

Chambers, E. (1987). Applied anthropology in the post-Vietnam era: Anticipations and ironies. *Annual Review of Anthropology, 16*, 309-337.

Clifford, J., & Marcus, G. (Eds.). (1986). *Writing culture: The poetics and politics of ethnography.* Berkeley: University of California Press.

Cook, T. D., & Campell, J. C. (1979). *Quasi-experimentation: Design and analysis issues for field settings.* Boston: Houghton-Mifflin.

Cross, W. E., Jr. (1990). Race and ethnicity: Effects on social networks. In M. Cochran et al. (Eds.), *Extending families: The social networks of parents and their children* (pp. 67-85). New York: Cambridge University Press.

Delgado-Gaitan, C. (1988). The value of conformity: Learning to stay in school. *Anthropology and Education Quarterly, 19*, 354-382.

Denzin, N. K. (1978). *The research act: A theoretical introduction to sociological method.* New York: McGraw-Hill.

205

Deyhle, D. E., Hess, G. A., & LeCompte, M. D. (1992). Approaching ethical issues for the qualitative researchers in education. In M. D. LeCompte, W. Millroy, & J. Preissle (Eds.), *The handbook of qualitative research in education* (pp. 595-642). San Diego, CA: Academic Press.

Dworkin, A. G. (1985). *When teachers give up: Teacher burnout, teacher turnover and their impact on children.* Austin, TX: The Hogg Foundation for Mental Health.

Dworkin, A. G. (1987). *Teacher burnout in the public schools: Structural causes and consequences for children.* Albany: State University of New York Press.

Fowler, F. J., & Mangione, T. W. (1990). *Standardized survey interviewing.* Newbury Park, CA: Sage.

Galaskiewicz, J., & Wasserman, S. (1993). Social network analysis: Concepts, methodology, and directions for the 1990s. *Sociological Methods & Research, 22,* 3-22.

Geertz, C. (1989-1990). *Works and lives: The anthropologist as author.* Stanford, CA: Stanford University Press.

Gibson, M. A. (1988). *Accommodation without assimilation: Punjabi Sikh immigrants in an American high school.* Ithaca, NY: Cornell University Press.

Glaser, B. G., & Strauss, A. L. (1967). *The discovery of grounded theory.* Chicago: Aldine.

Gonzalez, M., Schensul, J., Garcia, R., & Caro, E. (1982). Research, training and organizational change. *Urban Anthropology, 11,* 129-153.

Goodenough, W. H. (1956). Componential analysis and the study of meaning. *Language, 38,* 195-215.

Heath, S. B. (1996, September). *Postmodern narrative and its consequences in knowledge transmission.* Lecture #1 in a series of three presented at the University of Colorado, Boulder.

Henry, G. T. (1990). *Practical sampling.* Newbury Park, CA: Sage.

Jacob, E. (1987). Qualitative research: A defense of traditions. *Review of Educational Research, 59,* 229-235.

Jaeger, R. (1978). *Complementary methods.* Washington, DC: American Educational Research Association.

Johnson, J. C. (1994). Anthropological contributions to the study of social networks: A review. In S. Wasserman & J. Galaskiewicz (Eds.), *Advances in social network analysis.* Thousand Oaks, CA: Sage.

Kanani, S. J. (1992). Application of rapid assessment procedures in the context of women's morbidity: Experiences of a non-government organization in India. In N. S. Scrimshaw & G. R. Gleason (Eds.), *Rapid assessment procedures: Qualitative methodologies for planning and evaluation of health-related programmes* (pp. 123-136). Boston: INFDC.

LeCompte, M. D. (1975). Institutional constraints on teacher styles and the development of student work norms (Doctoral dissertation, University of Chicago, 1974). *Dissertation Abstracts International, 36,* 43A.

LeCompte, M. D. (1990). Review of *Designing Qualitative Research* by C. Marshal and G. P. Rossman. *Qualitative Studies in Education, 3,* 295-298.

LeCompte, M. D. (1994). Some notes on power, agenda and voice: A researcher's personal evolution toward critical collaborative research. In P.

McLaren & J. Giarelli (Eds.), *Critical theory and educational research* (pp. 92-112). Albany: State University of New York Press.

LeCompte, M. D. (1997). Trends in qualitative research methods. In L. Saha (Ed.), *International encyclopedia of the sociology of education.* Oxford, UK: Elsevier Sciences Ltd.

LeCompte, M. D., & McLaughlin, D. (1994). Witchcraft and blessings, science and rationality: Discourses of power and science in collaborative work with Navajo schools. In A. Gitlin (Ed.), *Power and method: Political activism and educational research* (pp. 147-166). New York: Routledge.

LeCompte, M. D., & Preissle J. P., with Tesch, R. (1993). *Ethnography and qualitative design in educational research* (2nd ed.). San Diego, CA: Academic Press.

Levine, R. J. (1998). The "best proven therapeutic method" standard in clinical trials in technologically developing countries. *IRB: A Review of Human Subjects Research, 20*(1), pp. 5-9. (Published by The Hastings Center, Garrison, NY 10524-5555)

Lincoln, Y. S., & Guba, E. G. (1985). *Naturalistic inquiry.* Beverly Hills, CA: Sage.

Lurie, P., & Wolfe, S. M. (1997). Unethical trials of interventions to reduce perinatal transmission of the human immunodeficiency virus in developing countries. *New England Journal of Medicine, 337,* 853-856.

Marcus, G. E., & Fischer, M. M. J. (1986). *Anthropology as cultural critique: An experimental moment in the human sciences.* Chicago: University of Chicago Press.

Martinez, E. L. (1998). *Valuing our differences: Contextual interaction factors that affect the academic achievement of Latino immigrant students in a K-5 elementary school.* Unpublished doctoral dissertation, University of Colorado, Boulder.

McDade, L. (1987). *Telling them what they do not want to know: A dilemma in ethnographic evaluation.* Paper presented at the annual meetings of the American Anthropological Association, Chicago.

McElroy, A., & Townsend, P. K. (1979). *Medical anthropology in ecological perspective.* North Scituate, MA: Duxbury Press.

McGrady, G. A., Marrow, C., Myers, G., Daniels, M., Vera, M., Mueller, C., Liebow, E. R., Klovdahl, A., & Lovely, R. (1995). A note on implementation of a random-walk design to study adolescent social networks. *Social Networks, 17, 251-255.*

McLaughlin, D., & Tierney, W. (1993). *Naming silenced lives: Personal narratives and the process of educational change.* New York: Routledge.

Merriman, S. B. (1988). *Case study research in education: A qualitative approach.* San Francisco: Jossey-Bass.

Milgram, S. (1963). Behavioral study of obedience. *Journal of Abnormal and Social Psychology, 67,* 371-378.

Mohanty, C. (1988). Under Western eyes: Feminist scholarship and colonial discourses. *Feminist Review, 30,* 60-88.

Nastasi, B. K., & Dezolt, D. M. (1994). *School interventions for children of alcoholics.* New York: Guilford.

Nastasi, B. K., Schensul, J., de Silva, M. W. A., Varjas, K., Silva, K. A., Ratnayake, P., & Schensul, S. (in press). Community-based sexual risk prevention program for Sri Lankan youth: Influencing sexual-risk decision making. *International Quarterly of Community Health Education.*

Needle, R. H., Coyle, S. L., Genser, S. G., & Trotter, R. T. (1995). Introduction: The social network paradigm. In R. H. Needle, S. L. Coyle, S. G. Genser, R. T. Trotter II (Eds.), *Social networks, drug abuse, and HIV transmission* (NIDA Research Monograph 151). Rockville, MD: NIDA.

O'Conor, A. (1993/1994). Who gets called queer in school? Lesbian, gay, and bisexual teenagers, homophobia and high school. *High School Journal, 77*(2), 7-13.

Pelto, P., & Gove, S. (1992). Developing a focused ethnographic study for the WHO Acute Respiratory Infection (ARI) Control Programme. In N. S. Scrimshaw & G. R. Gleason (Eds.), *RAP: Rapid assessment procedures: Qualitative methodologies for planning and evaluation of health-related programmes* (pp. 215-226). Boston: INFDC.

Pelto, P. J., & Pelto, G. H. (1978). *Anthropological research: The structure of inquiry* (2nd ed.). Cambridge: Cambridge University Press.

Phillips, E. (1996). Thinning out public housing residents. *Anthropology, 37,* 1(Newsletter). Arlington, VA: American Anthropological Association.

Poggie, J. J., Jr., DeWalt, B. R., & Dressler, W. W. (Eds.). (1992). *Anthropological research: Process and application.* Albany: State University of New York Press.

Porter, A. (1978). Experimental research design. In R. Jaeger (Ed.), *Complementary methods.* Washington, DC: American Educational Research Association.

Reichardt, C. S., & Cook, D. T. (1979). Beyond qualitative versus quantitative methods. In T. D. Cook & C. S. Reichardt (Eds.), *Qualitative and quantitative methods in evaluation research* (pp. 7-32). Beverly Hills, CA: Sage.

Rhoades, R. E. (1992). The coming revolution in methods for rural development research. In N. S. Scrimshaw & G. R. Gleason (Eds.), *RAP: Rapid assessment procedures: Qualitative methodologies for planning and evaluation of health-related programmes* (pp. 61-78). Boston: INFDC.

Romagnano, L. H. (1991). *Managing the dilemmas of change: A case study of two ninth grade general mathematics teachers.* Unpublished doctoral dissertation, University of Colorado, Boulder.

Said, E. (1978). *Orientalism.* New York: Pantheon.

Said, E. (1994). *Culture and imperialism.* New York: Knopf.

Schensul, J. J. (1998-1999). Learning about sexual meaning and decision-making from urban adolescents [Special issue]. *International Quarterly of Community Health Education, 18*(1), 29-48.

Schensul, J. (1999). Building community research partnerships in the struggle against AIDS [Special issue]. *Health Education and Behavior, 26,* 2.

Schensul, J. J., Berg, M., & Romero, M. (1997, July). *Using process evaluation to enhance facilitation skills in prevention staffing.* Invited paper presented at annual evaluation meeting of the Center for Substance Abuse Prevention, Washington, DC.

Schensul, J. J., Diaz, N., & Woolley, S. (1996, September). *Measuring activity levels among Puerto Rican children.* Paper presented at the 2nd Annual Puerto Rican Studies Association meetings, San Juan, Puerto Rico.

Schensul, J. J., & Eddy, E. M. (Eds.). (1985). Applying educational anthropology [Special issue]. *Anthropology and Education Quarterly, 16*(2).

Schensul, J. J., Oodit, G., Schensul, S. L., Seebuluk, S., Bhowan, V., Aukhojee, J. P., Rogobur, S., Koyekwat, B. L., & Affrock, S. (1994, June). *Young women, work and AIDS-related risk behavior in Mauritius* (Women and AIDS Research Program, Research in Report Series No. 2). Washington, DC: International Center for Research on Women.

Schensul, J. J., & Stern, G. (Eds.). (1985). Collaborative research and social policy. *American Behavioral Scientist, 29.*

Schensul, J., Radda, K., & Levy, J. (1999, June 11). *Building research partnerships for the study of AIDS risk exposure in older adults.* Paper presented at the annual meeting of the Society for Community Research and Action, Division 27 of the American Psychological Association. Yale University.

Schensul, S. L., & Schensul, J. J. (1978). Advocacy and applied anthropology. In G. H. Weber & G. McCall (Eds.), *Social scientists as advocates: Views from the applied disciplines* (pp. 121-166). Beverly Hills, CA: Sage.

Scrimshaw, S. C. M. (1992). The adaptation of anthropological methods to rapid assessment of nutrition and primary health care. In N. S. Scrimshaw & G. R. Gleason (Eds.), *RAP: Rapid assessment procedures: Qualitative methodologies for planning and evaluation of health-related programmes* (pp. 25-38). Boston: INFDC.

Scrimshaw, N. S., & Gleason, G. R. (Eds.). (1992). *RAP: Rapid assessment procedures: Qualitative methodologies for planning and evaluation of health-related programmes.* Boston: INFDC.

Scrimshaw, S. C. M., & Hurtado, E. (1985). *Rapid assessment procedures for nutrition and primary health care: Anthropological approaches to improving programme effectivness.* Tokyo: United Nations University.

Seeman, M. (1975). Alienation studies. *Annual Review of Sociology, 1,* 91-123.

Shepard, L. A., & Kreitzer, A. E. (1978, August/September). The Texas teacher test. *Educational Researcher,* pp. 22-31.

Singer, M. (1990). Another perspective on advocacy. *Current Anthropology, 31,* 548-549.

Society for Applied Anthropology. (1996). *Cooperative agreement with the EPA* (1996-01). Oklahoma City, OK: Author.

Spindler, G., & Spindler, L. (1992). Cultural process and ethnography: An anthropological perspective. In M. D. LeCompte, W. Millroy, & J. Preissle (Eds.), *The handbook of qualitative research in education* (pp. 53-92). San Diego, CA: Academic Press.

Spivak, G. C. (1988). Subaltern studies: Deconstructing historiography. In G. C. Spivak (Ed.), *In other worlds.* London: Routledge & Kegan Paul.

Spradley, J.P. (1979). *The ethnographic interview.* New York: NY: Holt, Rinehart & Winston.

Stringer, E. T. (1996). *Action research: A handbook for practitioners.* Thousand Oaks, CA: Sage.

Stull, D., & Schensul, J. J. (1987). *Collaborative research and social change.* Boulder, CO: Westview.

Trinh, M. T. T. (1989). *Woman, native, other: Writing on postcoloniality and feminism.* Bloomington: Indiana University Press.

Trotter, R. T., II, Baldwin, J. A., & Bowen, A. M. (1995). Network structure and proxy network measures of HIV, drug and incarceration risks for active drug users. *Connections, 18*(1), 89-104.

Trotter, R. T., II, Bowen, A. M., Baldwin, J. A., & Price, L. J. (1996). The efficacy of network based HIV/AIDS risk reduction programs in midsized towns in the United States. *Journal of Drug Issues, 26,* 591-606.

Trotter, R. T., II, Bowen, A. M., & Potter, J. M. (1995). Network models for HIV outreach and prevention programs of drug users. In R. H. Needle, S. L. Coyle, S. G. Genser, R. T. Trotter, II (Eds.), *Social networks, drug abuse, and HIV transmission* (NIDA Research Monograph 151, pp. 144-180). Rockville, MD: NIDA.

Trotter, R. T., II, Bowen, A. M., Potter, J. M., & Jiron, D. (1994). Enfoques ethnográficos y anlisis de las redes sociales, par la creación de programas de prevención del uso de drogas y de MIH, in usarios activos. In A. Rotiz (Ed.), *Las addicciones: Hacia un enfozue multidisciplinario.* Mexico City: Secretaría de Salud, Subsecretaría de Coordinación y Desarrollo, Consejo Nacional Contra las Addicciones.

Trotter, R. T., II, Rothenberg, R. B., & Coyle, S. (1995). Drug abuse and HIV prevention research: Expanding paradigms and network contributions to risk reduction. *Connections, 18*(1), 29-46.

Trotter, R. T., & Schensul, J. J. (1998). Research methods in applied anthropology. In H. R. Bernard (Ed.), *Handbook on methods in cultural anthropology.* Walnut Creek, CA: AltaMira.

Van Willigen, J. (1993). *Applied anthropology: An introduction.* Westport, CT: Bergin and Garvey.

Wasserman, S., & Faust, K. (Eds.). (1993). *Social network analysis: Methods and applications.* New York: Cambridge University Press.

Wax, R. H. (1971). *Doing fieldwork: Warnings and advice.* Chicago: University of Chicago Press.

Weeks, M., Schensul, J. J., Williams, M., & Singer, M. (1995). AIDS prevention for African-American and Latina women: Building culturally and gender appropriate intervention. *AIDS Education and Prevention, 7,* 251-264.

Weis, L., & Fine, M. (Eds.). (1993). *Beyond silenced voices: Class, race and gender in the United States.* Albany: State University of New York Press.

Whyte, W. F. (1991). *Participatory action research.* Newbury Park, CA: Sage.

Wolcott, H. F. (1987). *Writing up qualitative research.* Newbury Park, CA: Sage.

INDEX

ABOUT THE EDITORS, AUTHORS, AND ARTISTS

Jean J. Schensul is a medical/educational anthropologist. After completing her M.A. and Ph.D. at the University of Minnesota, she conducted intervention research in education at the Institute for Juvenile Research and Center for New Schools in Chicago. She served as co-founder and research director of the Hispanic Health Council in Hartford for ten years, and, since 1987, has been founder and executive director of the Institute for Community Research, based in Hartford, Connecticut, and dedicated to community-based partnership research. She has extensive experience in the use of ethnographic and survey research methods in the United States, Latin America, Southeast Asia, China, and West Africa. Her substantive interests are diverse, reflecting the contributions of ethnography to health, education, the arts, and community development. She co-edited three special journal issues on applied research in education, and policy, and, with Don Stull, a book titled *Collaborative Research and Social Change: Applied Anthro-*

pology in Action, and has published on other topics including substance abuse prevention, AIDS, adolescent development, chronic health problems, and the arts and community building. She is the recipient of a number of National Institute of Health Research grants, immediate past president of the Society for Applied Anthropology, former president of the Council on Anthropology and Education, and recipient (with Stephen Schensul) of the Kimball Award for Public Policy Research in Anthropology. She is adjunct professor of anthropology at the University of Connecticut and Senior Fellow, Department of Psychology, Yale University.

Margaret D. LeCompte is Professor of Education and Sociology in the School of Education, University of Colorado at Boulder. After completing her MA and PhD at the University of Chicago, she taught at the University of Houston and the University of Cincinnati, with visiting appointments at the University of North Dakota and the Universidad de Monterrey, Mexico. She also served as Executive Director for Research and Evaluation for the Houston public schools. In addition to many articles and book chapters, she cowrote *Ethnography and Qualitative Design in Educational Research* and coedited *The Handbook of Qualitative Research in Education,* the first textbook and first handbook, respectively, on ethnographic and qualitative methods in education. As a researcher, evaluator, and consultant to school districts, museums, and universities, she has published studies of dropouts, artistic and gifted students, school reform efforts, and the impact of strip mining on the social environment of rural communities. Fluent in Spanish, she is deeply interested in the education of language and ethnic minority children. She served as a Peace Corps volunteer in the Somali Republic from 1965 to 1967.

Ed Johnetta Miller is a weaver/silk painter/gallery curator/quilter and Master Teaching Artist. Her work has appeared in the *New York Times* and *FiberArts Magazine* and in the Renwick Gallery of the Smithsonian, American Crafts Museum, and Wadsworth Atheneum. She is the Director of OPUS, Inc., Co-Director of the Hartford Artisans Center, and consultant to Aid to Artisans, Ghana. She teaches workshops on weaving, silk painting and quilting to children and adults throughout the United States.

Graciela Quiñones Rodriguez is a folk artist, carving *higueras* (gourds) and working in clay, wood, and lithographs with symbols and icons derived from Taino and other indigenous art forms. She builds *cuatros, tiples,* and other Puerto Rican folk instruments guided by the inspiration of her grandfather Lile and her uncle Nando who first introduced her to Puerto Rican cultural history and Taino culture and motifs. Her work has been exhibited in major galleries thoughout Connecticut, at the Bridgeport Public Library, and at the Smithsonian Institute.